English for Travel

OXFORD UNIVERSITY PRESS

English for Travel

JOHN EASTWOOD

Oxford University Press
Walton Street, Oxford OX2 6DP

Oxford New York Toronto
Delhi Bombay Calcutta Madras
Karachi Petaling Jaya Singapore
Hong Kong Tokyo Nairobi
Dar es Salaam Cape Town
Melbourne Auckland

and associated companies in
Berlin Ibadan

Oxford, Oxford English and the
Oxford English logo are
trademarks of Oxford University Press
ISBN 0 19 451305 X
© John Eastwood 1980

First published 1980
Seventh impression 1989

Photographs by
Terry Williams
Mark Mason

Cover illustration by
David Scutt

Printed in Yugoslavia

Contents

Introduction

English for Travel is a course for business people and tourists. It is for people who travel to English-speaking countries or to countries where English is often used at airports, in restaurants, in shops and so on. It is a practical course which teaches you how to use English when buying a ticket, ordering a meal, hiring a car etc.

The course tells the story of a business trip to Athens. Peter and Maria Almar have a shop in Zurich. They visit Istanbul and Athens to buy things for their shop, and they also have a few days' holiday in Greece.

English for Travel can be used as a self-study course – you can use it at home without a teacher. (It can also be used with a teacher, and there is a Teacher's Guide to help teachers use the course in the classroom.) You must know a little English before you start the course. (You may have learnt some at school or have spent one or two years learning English at evening classes.) There are explanations of the more difficult or important words in each unit (Key Words) and an alphabetical Wordlist at the back of this book (pages 107–113). This will help you to find an explanation quickly if you do not know the meaning of a word.

Many words that the traveller needs are different in British English and American English. Both British and American English words are given in the Key Words and Wordlist.

The parts of the course are this book (the Coursebook) and two cassettes, so you will need a cassette player. The cassettes are a very important part of the course because the traveller has to do a lot of listening and speaking. The cassettes help you to listen to and understand English as it is used by travel agents, shop assistants etc. They also give you the chance to practise the kind of sentences you need to say when you have to ask for information, buy things etc. *English for Travel* teaches *useful* English; it teaches *realistic* English; and it gives *active* practice in the English needed for travel.

◁ *The Almars' shop in Zurich*

To find out what English the traveller needs to understand and to use, we took recordings of travel agents, shop assistants etc. The English in the Listening for Information is taken from these recordings.

How to use the course

The course is in 11 units, each about a different aspect of travel – 'Asking about travel', 'At a hotel' etc. It is best if you work through the units from 1 to 11. If you already know a lot of English, you can leave out some units and do only those that you are most interested in or that are most useful to you. However, a lot of things in the course (e.g. how to ask questions) can be used in different situations, and so it will normally be best for you to work through the whole course.

Instructions for using the material are given in each unit of this book and on the cassettes. But here is a list of the parts of each unit with suggestions as to how they should be used.

1 Dialogue

The Dialogue tells the story of the Almars' trip to Athens. In the Dialogue there are examples of the language that you will practise in the unit. Listen to the Dialogue and try to understand it without looking at the words in your book. If you cannot understand the Dialogue at first, read it in your book and find out the meaning of the unknown words from the Key Words, which are after the Dialogue. Play the Dialogue again until you can understand it without looking at your book. When you understand the Dialogue, practise saying Peter's or Maria's words after the words on the tape.

2 Key words

The more difficult or more important words from the Dialogue and from the Listening for Information are listed here with an explanation or example. These words are also in the Wordlist at the back of the book so that if you forget the meaning of a word, you can find it quickly later on. When you have finished a unit, look back again at the Key Words you have learnt.

3 Using the language

The first two exercises help you to practise some of the
phrases and grammar in the Dialogue. You practise
saying what you want, asking questions etc. These
exercises are on your cassette, and the answers are all
given too, so that you can check that your answer is
correct. Always try to speak like the voice on the
cassette. It is best if you do not look at your book when
you are saying the answers, but you should look at your
book if you find the sentences too difficult at first.

The third exercise is a short dialogue in which you
play the role of a traveller, customer etc. at a travel
agency, bank or shop. First you listen to the dialogue;
secondly, you say the traveller's words at the same time
as he or she says them; and thirdly, you have to stop the
tape when it is the traveller's turn to speak, and you
have to say the traveller's words. You can look at the
words in your book until you are ready to play your role
from memory.

4 Listening for information

This part of the unit contains a conversation (recorded
on cassette), and a number of written questions about
the conversation. In each conversation the words of the
travel agent, shop assistant etc. are taken from a real
conversation, so you will hear *real* English, the English
you have to understand in real life. This means that you
may find the conversation difficult to understand when
you first hear it, but your work on the Dialogue and on
Using the Language will help you. Try to understand the
conversation first without looking at your book, but if
you find it difficult, follow the words in your book as
you listen. Some of the words were also in the Dialogue,
others you will find in the Key Words. But remember
that you do not need to understand every word. The
important thing is to understand the meaning of the
whole phrase or sentence. Listen to the conversation
again until you can understand it without looking at
your book. When you understand the conversation, read
the questions in your book. Then play the conversation
again, listening for the information that you need to
answer the questions. Stop the tape and write the answer

to each question or group of questions; or take notes on
a piece of paper as you listen, and then write all the
answers when the conversation has finished. Answer
each question in a word or short phrase. It is important
that you do *not* read the conversation after you have
looked at the questions, because the questions are a test
of *listening*. Check your answers with the Key
(pages 104–106).

5 Reading for information

The traveller has to understand spoken information, and
written information too. You hear real English spoken in
the Listening for Information, and in this part of the unit
the brochure, timetable etc. is a *real* brochure or a *real*
timetable. As with listening, the important thing when
reading is to find the information you want. You do not
need to understand every word the first time. You must
answer the questions by finding the information from the
written material. The more difficult words are explained
in the Notes, but try to answer the questions before
looking at the Notes if you can. Look at the Key
to make sure your answers are correct.

Additional notes

In one unit (Unit 3) there is also a writing exercise on
filling in a form.

When you are learning English, it is best to work for not
more than 1–1½ hours at one time. Two lessons of half
an hour are better than one lesson of one hour. Practise
as often as you can – two or three times a week, or
every day. This is much better than, for example,
spending a period of 4 or 5 hours on the course every
month.

After each unit look again at the Key Words and try to
remember a sentence with each word. If you found a
unit difficult, do it again – it will be easier the second
time. Or you can come back to it again later. The more
you practise, the better your English will be.

Acknowledgements

The author and publishers would like to thank the following for their assistance and co-operation with the preparation of source recordings:

Waye and Son, Otley
Norfolk Gardens Hotel, Bradford
Schofields Ltd, Leeds
Oxford Travel Agency

H.M. Customs, Luton Airport
British Airways
Jane Calin
Tim Hodlin

Dept. of Language and Literature, College of Ripon and York St. John

The author would like to thank Sheila Eastwood for help with transcription and typing and Peter Donovan of OUP for help with collection of recordings and course planning.

The publisher would like to thank the following for permission to base a number of illustrations on their publicity material:

British Rail Hovercraft Ltd.
H.M. Customs and Excise
The Two Sisters Restaurant, Ilkley
Diners Club Ltd.

The Post Office
English Tourist Board
London Transport
Bricar Overseas Car Rental
Miles Laboratories Ltd.

The publishers wish to acknowledge the following for permission to reproduce photographs:

Photographs lent by agencies
The Sport and General Press
Post Office
Farmers Weekly
British Railways Board
Poultry World
Cherry Valley Farms Ltd.

Fleet PR
Leyland Vehicles Ltd.
Ford Motor Company Ltd.
Lotus Cars (Sales) Ltd.
London Transport Executive
Armitage Shanks Sales Ltd.

Assistance with photographs was provided by
Terracotta (Oxford)
Russell & Bromley Ltd.
Lyndon Jewellers Ltd.
Pamela Meads Model Agency
City Motors (Oxford)
Ducker & Son Ltd.
Frida

CBA Travel Services
Pan American World Airlines
Dorchester Hotel
Ritz Hotel
Avis Rent-a-Car
Katrina

Unit 1   Asking about travel

Dialogue

Listen to the Dialogue. If you need to, you can look at the words in your book or at the Key Words after the Dialogue.

Peter and Maria Almar are in Istanbul, where they are buying things for their shop in Zurich. They want to talk to the manager of an export company, but he is not there at the moment, so the Almars plan to go to Athens for three days and then back to Istanbul. Peter is enquiring at a travel agency about travel to Athens.

Peter   Good morning. I want to go to Athens. Could you tell me if there's a train today or tomorrow?

Travel agent   There's a train every evening at 22.30.

Peter   What time does it arrive in Athens, please?

Travel agent   The train leaving today arrives at 11.40 on Wednesday.

Peter   How much does it cost?

Travel agent   The single fare is TL848 first class and TL567 second class.

Peter   Sleeping accommodation is included, is it?

Travel agent   No, that's extra.

Peter   Oh. What sort of accommodation is there?

Travel agent   Well, that depends on whether you travel first or second class. There are single-berth compartments for first-class passengers and two or three-berth compartments for second-class passengers.

Peter   How much is a first-class berth?

Travel agent   TL425 each night.

Peter   Can I book a berth in advance?

Travel agent   Yes, we can book a berth for you, providing there's space, of course.

Peter   I see. And how much is it to Athens by air, please? Tourist class.

Travel agent   TL1699. There's a flight tomorrow at 17.50 that gets to Athens at 18.40.

Peter   Is there any reduction for a return journey?

Travel agent   No, it's double fare, the same each way.

Peter   Well, I'll have to think about it first. I'll call back
  to book the tickets. Thank you.
Travel agent   Thank you, sir.

Go back and listen again to the
Dialogue until you can understand it
without looking at the words. Then
practise saying Peter's words after him.

①   ②

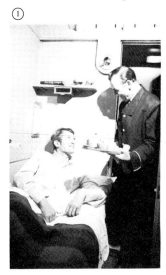

Compartments
1   First class
2   Second class
3   Berth

Key words

accommodation *place for sleeping*
adult *person who is no longer a
  child*
in advance *before*
berth *bed in a boat*
book *buy tickets for a seat, berth
  etc. in advance*
cabin *a room on a boat*
call back *come back; (when on the
  telephone) telephone again*
compartment *a room on a train*
couchette *bed in a train
  compartment or boat*

depend on *How much the meal costs
  depends on what you eat.*
double *×2*
each way *for both journeys*
enquire *ask*
fare *money paid for a journey*
ferry *boat*
flight *journey by air*
following *next*
include *Meals aren't included;
  they're extra.*
involve *be part of something*
passenger *person who is travelling*

providing *if*
reduction *making less*
reservation *booking in advance*
return (USA: round trip/two way)
  going to a place and back again
shower *I'd like a bath or shower.*
single ×1
single (USA: one way) *going to a
place but not coming back*

space *an empty place not already
  booked*
special *having something extra*
toilet (USA: bathroom/rest
  room) *WC*
travel agency *shop where you buy
  travel tickets*
wash-basin (USA: washbowl) *You
  wash your hands in a wash-basin.*

Using the language

Asking for information

Listen to the examples on your tape
and then try to do the exercise
without looking at your book. You
will hear each correct answer after
you say it.

1 You want to know if there's a train from Stockholm
to Malmö.
*Could you tell me if there's a train from Stockholm to
Malmö, please?*
2 You want to know where the toilet is.
Could you tell me where the toilet is, please?

You want to know	how much it costs to fly to Tokyo.
	how much a letter to France costs.
	if there's a bus to the airport.
	what time breakfast is.
	when the next train leaves.
	if you can book a seat in advance.

Checking information

Listen to the information and then
check that it is correct by making
sentences with *is it?* or *are they?*

1 Sleeping accommodation is included.
Sleeping accommodation is included, is it?
2 The prices are for second class.
The prices are for second class, are they?
3 It's a three-hour journey.
4 These are return tickets.

5 A berth is extra.
6 Couchettes are cheaper.
7 Two-berth compartments are more expensive.
8 It's double fare for the return journey.

At a travel agency
Listen to this dialogue.

Travel agent   Can I help you?
Traveller   *Could you tell me if there's a bus from Chicago to Cleveland in the morning?*
Travel agent   They're at 6.30, 8.00 and 9.50.
Traveller   *What time does the 8.00 arrive in Cleveland?*
Travel agent   It gets into Cleveland at 4.05.
Traveller   *And how much does it cost?*
Travel agent $26·25.
Traveller   *Well, I'll call back. I'll have to think about it first.*
Travel agent   You buy your ticket on the bus.
Traveller   *I see. Thank you.*

Go back and play the role of the traveller. Say the traveller's words at the same time as she does. You can look at your book if you need to. Now go back again and this time play the role of the traveller without looking at your book. Stop the tape after the travel agent's words and say the traveller's words.

Listening for information

Now you will hear a conversation in which a traveller asks for information. Listen to the conversation and try to understand it without looking at the words in your book or at the Key Words on pages 3 and 4.

Traveller   Good morning. Could you tell me if there's a night ferry from Hull to Rotterdam?
Travel agent   Yes, it's six o'clock every evening.
Traveller   And what time does it get into Rotterdam?

Travel agent   Eight o'clock the following morning.
Traveller   Uh-huh. There's just the one ferry, is there?
Travel agent   Yes, it goes at six o'clock every evening.
Traveller   Uh-huh. And how much does it cost?
Travel agent   That depends on the sort of
accommodation. How many passengers are there?
Traveller   Well, we're two adults and two children, and
we'd like a cabin. What sort of accommodation is
there on the boat?
Travel agent   Well, there's either a two-berth cabin – a
two-berth standard cabin – what time of year?
Traveller   We're going in July.
Travel agent   July. Well, for a standard cabin that
would be £32, that's per person, and for a special
cabin, which has got wash-basin, shower and toilet,
that'd be £36 per person. It's half fare for the
children, under twelve.
Traveller   Oh, I see. Well, they're both over twelve.
Travel agent   Oh, well, they're both full then. So that'd
be four adults. So, as I say, up to the end of
September a special cabin is £36 and a standard
cabin is £32, or there are couchette cabins which are
a bit cheaper, that's £25·80.
Traveller   £25·80.
Travel agent   And that's just for the passengers, that's

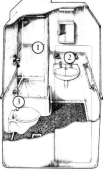

single journey, and that includes dinner, berth and
breakfast, so there's two meals involved as well as
the accommodation.

1   *Shower*
2   *Washbasin*
3   *Toilet*

Traveller   And the car is extra, is it?
Travel agent   Yes, the car depends on the length. What
make is it?
Traveller   Oh, it's a Datsun 240. I don't know how
long it is.
Travel agent   And the year? Datsun 240. What year is it?
Traveller   78.
Travel agent   That'd be £31·60 each way.
Traveller   £31·60.
Travel agent   Yes.
Traveller   Is there any reduction for a return journey?
Travel agent   No, it's just a straight double.
Traveller   So it would be four times whatever type of
cabin we have, from £36 down to £25·80, plus the
£31·60 for the car, each way.

Travel agent   Each way. That's right, yes.
Traveller   And what about reservations? Do you have
to book well in advance?
Travel agent   Well, providing there's space, we can get
you on the same day, but we do have to enquire for
each one, you know.
Traveller   OK. Well, thank you very much. I'll probably
call back to book the tickets. I'll have to think about
it first.
Travel agent   OK. Thank you, sir.

Go back and listen again to the
conversation until you can understand it without looking at the words.
When you understand it, read the
questions in your book. Then
play the conversation again, and
stop the tape to write the answer
to each question. Do not read the
conversation in your book when you
are answering the questions.

1 What time in the evening does the ferry leave Hull?
2 What time does it arrive in Rotterdam?
3 How many people can sleep in a standard cabin?
4 How much does a standard cabin cost per person?
5 What three things are there in a special cabin but not
in a standard cabin?
6 How much does a special cabin cost per person?
7 At what age do children pay the full fare?
8 What are the cheapest cabins called?
9 How much do they cost per person?
10 Does the fare include dinner?
11 Does it include breakfast?
12 Does it include the car?
13 How much is the return fare?
   a) $1\frac{1}{2}$ × the single fare.   b) 2 × the single fare.
14 Does the travel agent have to phone the company
before she can sell a ticket?

Now check your answers with the
Key on page 104.

Reading for information

Look at the information and then answer the questions. Use the Notes if you need to, but try to answer the questions before looking at the Notes if you can.

Vehicle Rates

Rates shown are for single journeys and are applicable to the actual date of travel, return rates are double.
SPECIAL REDUCTION: The summer peak vehicle Tariff (covering journeys on Fridays and Saturdays 15 July to 27 August inclusive) will NOT be applied to bookings made and paid for prior to 1 May.

Cars, coaches mini-buses, caravans and trailers

Length of Vehicle not exceeding	Standard 1 Jan-3 July 5 Sept-31 Dec	Summer 4 July-4 Sept	Summer Peak Fri & Sat only 15 July-27 Aug
3.8m (12′ 6″)	£13.00	£16.60	£19.20
4.3m (14′ 1″)	£18.00	£23.10	£26.70
4.7m (15′ 5″)	£23.70	£30.50	£35.20

Over 4.7m (15′ 5″): Supplementary charge per 30 cms (1 foot) in excess.

	£ 2.25	£ 2.70	£ 3.15
Motorcycle combinations	£13.00	£16.60	£19.20
Motorcycles	£ 4.50	£ 5.40	£ 6.30
Bicycles	£ 2.00	£ 2.40	£ 2.80

Motorcycle combinations, motorcycles and bicycles are not reservable in advance, bookable at Seaspeed Dover on day of travel only.

Passengers travelling with vehicles

	Standard 1 Jan-3 July 5 Sept-31 Dec	Summer 4 July-4 Sept	Summer Peak Fri & Sat only 15 July-27 Aug
Adult	£8.60	£8.60	£8.60
Child (4 to 13 yrs)	£4.30	£4.30	£4.30

General Information

Motorists should check in at least 45 minutes before departure time at the Hoverports at Dover or Boulogne or Calais.

Always book in advance if possible.

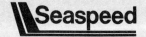

1 What is the *single* fare for a car 4·5 metres long
travelling on Thursday 21st July?
2 What is the *return* fare for a car 3·5 metres long
travelling in June?
3 How can you travel at the summer peak time but not
pay the summer peak rate?
a) If you book before 1 May.
b) If you book before 15 July.
4 Does a 14-year-old child pay half fare or full fare?
5 Your hovercraft leaves at 10.30. What is the latest
time you can arrive at the Hoverport?

Now check your answers with the
Key on page 104.

Notes

actual *real*
apply to/be applicable to *The extra
fare is applicable to first-class
passengers only and will not be paid
by second-class passengers.*
charge *money that you are asked to
pay*
check in *arrive at an airport, bus
station etc. and show your ticket*
cover *be applicable to*
departure time *time when the bus,
ferry etc. leaves*
exceed/be in excess *be more than*
general information *information for
all travellers*

hoverport *place where hovercraft
arrive and leave*
motorcycle combination *motorcycle
and sidecar*
peak *time when most people travel*
prior to *before*
rate *charge*
service *something arranged for
travellers: The bus service to the
town is poor, but the train service is
good.*
supplementary *extra*
tariff *charge*
trailer *something pulled by a vehicle*
vehicle *car, bus etc.*

1 *Coach*
(USA: bus)
2 *Motorcycle*
3 *Car*
4 *Caravan*
(USA: trailer)

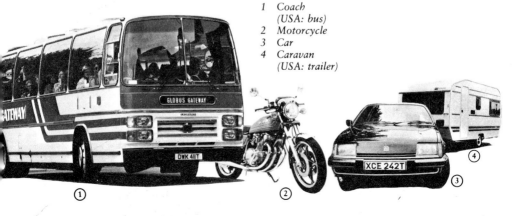

① ② ③ ④

Unit 2   Making travel arrangements

```
1 PA 101 Y  15MAY  LHRJFK HS1      1200 1335◢
2 PA 103 Y  16MAY  JFKLAX HS1      2100 2325◢
3 PA 811 Y  21MAY  LAXAKL HS1      2015 0745◢
4 PA 812 Y  31MAY  AKLLAX HS1      2130 1705◢
5 PA 120 Y   2JUN  LAXLHR HS1      1830 1335◢
RCVD/RLOC-PSGR◢
FONE-LON-D 759 2595◢
TKT-001FEBLON016B1◢
▶PSGR RQSTS NON SMOKING AISLE SEAT◢
FREQUENT PAN AM PASSENGER ◢
TO BE SEATED WITH PARTY 2JACKSON LAX/AKL/LAX SEGMENTS◢
ADVISED OF ALL TRAVEL DOCUMENTS◢
█

NYC STATION INFORMATION                                  01FEB
                        AIRPORT◢
     ## MOVE DOWN ## FOR NA INFO                               .
                                                              .
     KENNEDY INTL   - 16 MILES FROM CITY    CHECK-IN 60 MIN   .
                                                              .
     CONNECTING TIME IN MINUTES                               .
     BTWN DOM SVC/ FROM DOM TO INTL/ FROM INTL TO DOM/ BTWN INTL.
          60*          75**              105###        120####.
                                                              .
     #......PA DOMESTIC TO PA DOMESTIC - 40MIN                 .
                                                              .
     ##.....AL TO PA - 45MIN                                  .
     ###....PA TO AL - 60MIN                                  .
 #▶                                                           .
```

Dialogue

Listen to the Dialogue. If you need to, you can look at the words in your book or at the Key Words after the Dialogue.

Peter and Maria Almar decide to go to Athens by air. Maria goes to the travel agency to book the tickets.

Maria   Good afternoon. I'd like to book two return air tickets from Istanbul to Athens, please.

Travel agent   Certainly. When are you travelling?

Maria   We want to take the flight tomorrow afternoon and come back next Friday afternoon.

Travel agent   First class or economy class?

Maria   Economy class.

Travel agent   Two adults?

Maria   Yes.

Travel agent   And your name is . . .?

Maria   Almar. A-L-M-A-R.

Travel agent   Initials?

Maria   M. H.

Travel agent   And the other passenger?

Maria   P. J. Almar.

Travel agent   On the 11th and the 14th, did you say?

Maria   That's right. Do we have to change?

Travel agent   No, it's a direct flight. Here are your tickets, Mrs Almar. These are for the outward journey – Istanbul to Athens on flight SN 862 at 17.50 on 11th July. And these are for the return journey – Athens to Istanbul on SN 863 at 15.10 on 14th July. Don't forget to be at the airport 45 minutes before departure time.

Maria   Thank you. Do you accept credit cards?

Travel agent   Certainly. Thank you. That's TL6796. Could you sign here, please? Thank you very much.

Maria   Thank you.

Credit card

Go back and listen again to the Dialogue until you can understand it without looking at the words. Then practise saying Maria's words after her.

Key words

accept *accept dollars = allow a person to pay in dollars*

apart from *You can travel any day apart from Friday = you can't travel on Friday.*

approximately *about: The flight takes approximately 10 hours.*

arrangements *make arrangements = make plans, get ready*

available *can be used*

'cause *because*

certainly *yes, of course*

change *The ticket was $4·50. I paid $5 and got 50¢ change.*

change *get into a different plane, train etc. in the middle of a journey*

conditions of this ticket *what you are allowed and not allowed to do after buying the ticket*

copy *I have a copy of my letter to the hotel.*

credit card *e.g. an American Express card*

decide *choose: After thinking about it, I decided to go by bus.*

direct flight *flight on which you do not need to change*

economy class *second class*

initials *John David Smith's initials are J. D. S.*

monthly return *return ticket for trips up to one month*

ordinary *normal, standard*

outward journey *first part of a return journey*

probably *I'll probably leave tomorrow = I think I'll leave tomorrow.*

rail ticket *train ticket*

restriction *There's a restriction on exporting money. You can only take out £100.*

sign *write your name*

slightly *a little*

surcharge *make an extra charge*

via *Auckland to Delhi via Melbourne and Hong Kong*

Using the language

Saying what you want

Listen to the examples on your tape and then try to do the exercise without looking at your book. You will hear each correct answer after you say it.

1 You want to make a reservation.
   I'd like to make a reservation, please.
2 You want to buy a ticket for the ferry to Barcelona.
   I'd like to buy a ticket for the ferry to Barcelona, please.

	book a cabin.
	have a shower.
You want to	book a single room for 10th August.
	book a table for this evening.
	have some US dollars.
	buy an air ticket to Nairobi.

Asking what you must do

Listen to the examples and then you
ask the questions.

1 You don't know if you have to change planes or not.
  Do I have to change planes?
2 You don't know if you have to book in advance or
  not.
  Do I have to book in advance?

	book a table or not.
	have a visa or not.
You don't know	pay in advance or not.
if you have to	sign the copy or not.
	write your address or not.
	make the arrangements now or later.

At a travel agency

Listen to this dialogue.

Travel agent Good afternoon.
Traveller *Good afternoon. I'd like a rail ticket to
Amsterdam, please.*
Travel agent Certainly. When are you travelling?
Traveller *I'm taking the four o'clock train today.*
Travel agent First or second class?
Traveller *First class, please.*
Travel agent That's £82·25, please.
Traveller *Do you accept credit cards?*
Travel agent Certainly. Thank you. Sign here, please.
  Thank you very much.
Traveller *Thank you.*

Go back and play the role of the
traveller. Say the traveller's words at
the same time as he does. You can
look at your book if you need to.

Now go back again and this time
play the role of the traveller without
looking at your book. Stop the tape
after the travel agent's words and say
the traveller's words.

Listening for information

Now you will hear a conversation in
which a traveller buys a ticket. Listen
to the conversation and try to
understand it without looking at the
words in your book or at the Key
Words on page 12.

Traveller   Do you sell rail tickets?
Travel agent   Yes, certainly.
Traveller   I need a return ticket from Leeds to
  Colchester. I'm going on Sunday and coming back
  next Friday.
Travel agent   That'll be a monthly return actually,
  which is slightly less expensive than the ordinary
  return. Colchester, that's via London?
Traveller   Yes.
Travel agent   It's £19·00 as far as London and an extra
  £5·55 through to Colchester.
Traveller   £24·55.
Travel agent   £24·55, yes.
Traveller   Can I travel on any trains I like with that
  ticket?
Travel agent   Well, there's no restriction apart from
  coming back; on the Thursday you said, didn't you?
Traveller   No, Friday.
Travel agent   Friday. Oh, well, there are restrictions
  coming back on a Friday. It depends what time
  you're going to come back – in the morning or
  afternoon?

Tickets

Traveller   Afternoon. I'll probably want to come back
   on either the 19.00 or the 19.40 from London.
Travel agent   The 19.40's OK.
Traveller   But not the 19.00?
Travel agent   No.
Traveller   Would I have to pay extra on that one?
Travel agent   If you came back on the 19.00, they'd
   surcharge you up to the normal fare, which would be
   approximately . . . about £4 extra to pay.
Traveller   Oh, well, I'll take the cheaper one then.
Travel agent   There's no restriction going down, and
   the only conditions of this ticket are that if you
   travel . . . well, if you travel on a Sunday, you're OK
   'cause it's available for return on or after the
   following day, Monday, so you're OK. Where you
   can't use it is if you were going down on the
   Monday, for example, you couldn't return on the
   Friday, you'd have to wait till the Saturday.
Traveller   Well, I'll take the cheaper one then, the one
   at £24·55.
Travel agent   Monthly return to Colchester. One adult.
   £24·55. And you're travelling on the . . .?
Traveller   Sunday.
Travel agent   Sunday the 19th?
Traveller   Yes.

Railway station
(USA: train station)
1   *Engine*
    (USA: locomotive)
2   *Carriage*
    (USA: car)
1+2   *Train*
3   *Platform*

Travel agent That's your ticket. That one's for the outward journey, as it says there, Leeds to Colchester, and the copy is to bring you back.
Traveller Thank you.
Travel agent Thank you very much. And 45 pence change.
Traveller Thank you.

Go back and listen again to the conversation until you can understand it without looking at the words. When you understand it, read the questions in your book. Then play the conversation again, and stop the tape to write the answer to each question. Do not read the conversation in your book when you are answering the questions.

1 Which is cheaper, a monthly return or an ordinary return?
2 What is the monthly return fare for the whole journey?
3 On part of the journey there is a train you cannot use with a monthly return ticket. Is it on the outward or the return journey?
4 What time is the train you cannot use?
5 How much extra would it cost to travel on any train you like?
6 If the outward journey is on *Sunday*, what is the first day that the return journey is allowed?
7 If the outward journey is on *Monday*, what is the first day you can come back?
8 Is the *copy* of the ticket for the outward or the return journey?

Now check your answers with the Key on page 104.

Reading for information

Look at the information and then
answer the questions. Use the Notes
if you need to, but try to answer the
questions before looking at the Notes
if you can.

General information

Baggage (free allowance)

The free allowance for each adult or child
paying half fare is:

On International Journeys—Tourist Class
44 lb. (20 kgs) First Class 66 lb. (30 kgs.)
On Domestic Services 33 lb. (15 kgs)

There is no Free Allowance for an infant
carried at 10 per cent of the adult fare, but
infants food for consumption in flight and an
infants' carrying basket are carried free of
charge. Baggage in excess of the Free
Allowance is charged for per kilogram at the
rate of 1% of the one way, normal, adult,
direct, first class, through fare and on
domestic services 1% of the respective
class fare paid.

Children

An infant under two years of age travelling
on International Services accompanied by
an adult and not occupying a separate seat

is carried at 10% of the adult fare. Additional
infants under two years of age
accompanying the same adult, infants
under two years of age occupying a
separate seat and children of two years of
age and above, but under twelve years of
age are carried at 50% of the adult fare.

Youth fares

A discount of 25% of the normal tourist
single, return or excursion fare is available
to young people under the age of twenty
two. Full information obtainable on request.

Airport service charges

In some countries an airport service charge,
payable locally before departure is levied on
all passengers embarking on International
Flights.
The charge levied on passengers (except
children under two years of age and
passengers in transit) embarking from
Yugoslavia is: Y.D. 35

Road transport

Transport between town terminal and airport
is available at the following charge:–
Pula   Y.D. 15.00   Split   Y.D. 20.00
Zagreb Y.D. 15.00   Belgrade Y.D. 15.00
Dubrovnik Y.D. 20.00   Ljubjana Y.D. 20.00
Time of reporting at the airport. Passengers
must report at the check-in desk and have
all formalities completed 30 minutes before
aircraft departure. Departures cannot be
delayed for passengers who arrive late.

1 How much baggage is an international tourist-class
passenger allowed to take without extra charge?
2 How much would it cost an international tourist-class
passenger to take 5 kilograms of excess baggage?
   a) 1% of the tourist-class fare.
   b) 5% of the tourist-class fare.
   c) 5% of the first-class fare.
3 What is the fare for a 4-year-old child?
   a) No charge.
   b) 10% of the full fare.
   c) Half fare.
4 At what age are youth fares no longer available?
5 When do you pay the airport service charge?
   a) When you buy your ticket.
   b) When you catch your plane.
6 How much is the airport charge?
7 How much does it cost to travel from the terminal in
Belgrade to the airport?
8 Your plane leaves at 11.15. What is the latest time
you can check in?

Baggage

Now check your answers with the
Key on page 104.

Notes

accompany *travel with*
additional *more, extra*
aircraft (USA: airplane) *plane*
allowance *baggage allowance = how
  much baggage you are allowed to
  take*
charge *ask somebody to pay money*
complete *finish*
consumption *eating*
delay an aircraft *keep an aircraft
  waiting*
discount *reduction in price*
domestic *inside a country, not
  international*
embark *get on a plane or ship*
formalities *things that always have
  to be done e.g. showing your ticket
  and passport*
infant *young child*
lb *pound = 0·454 kilograms*
levy a charge *ask somebody to pay
  money*
locally *payable locally = which can
  be paid at that place*
obtainable *which you can have*
occupy a seat *sit in a seat*
on request *if you ask*
respective fare *fare which was paid,
  fare which applies*
separate *different*
terminal *place in a town where
  buses leave for the airport*
in transit *in the middle of a journey*
youth *young person*

Unit 3　At an airport

Flight arrivals

Arrivals		from	last stop	due	
	QF 002	SYDNEY	BOMBAY	11:35	01:00
	PA 282	LOS ANGELES		13:05	17:20
	MS 779	CAIRO		15:05	15:20
	ME 201	BEIRUT		15:25	15:25
	RJ 111	AMMAN		15:30	15:30
	BA 150	CAIRO		15:35	15:50
	SV 173	DHAHRAN	GENEVA	15:40	15:30
	WT 802	LAGOS	KANO	17:35	18:25

Passengers ending their journey in this terminal normally leave
the Customs Hall approximately 60 minutes after the time of landing

Dialogue

Listen to the Dialogue. If you need
to, you can look at the words in
your book or at the Key Words after
the Dialogue.

Peter and Maria Almar have
arrived at Istanbul airport to catch a
plane to Athens.

Maria   Is this the check-in for the flight to Athens?
Check-in clerk   Yes, that's right. Can I see your tickets
and passports, please? And could you put your
baggage on the scale?
Peter   Can I take this briefcase as hand baggage?
Check-in clerk   Yes, that's all right. Smoking or no
smoking?
Maria   No smoking, please.
Check-in clerk   Here are your boarding cards. You'll
need to show them again at the gate.
Maria   Can we board the aircraft now?
Check-in clerk   Can you wait until it's announced,
please, and then go to Passport Control.
Announcement   Sabena Airways flight SN 862 to
Athens and Brussels. This flight is now boarding at
Gate 6.
Check-in clerk   Boarding now at Gate 6.
Maria   Thank you.

1   *Visa*
2   *Passport*
3   *Boarding card*
4   *Ticket*

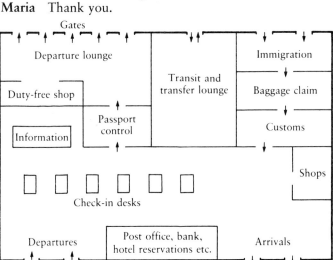

At Passport Control Peter has to answer some questions.

Passport officer Do you live in Switzerland?
Peter Yes, I do.
Passport officer What was the purpose of your visit to
   Turkey?
Peter It was a business trip.
Passport officer Was this your first visit?
Peter No, I've been here twice before.
Passport officer Have you got a
   vaccination certificate for cholera?
Peter Yes, I've got it here.
Passport officer OK, thank you.

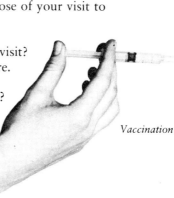

Vaccination

Go back and listen again to the
Dialogue until you can understand it
without looking at the words. Then
practise saying Peter and Maria's
words after them.

Key words

above *more than*
I'm afraid *I'm sorry to say*
announce/make an announcement
  give information to a group of
  people
as long as *if*
board *get on a plane, ship, train etc.*
briefcase *small case for papers*
cholera *illness you can catch in hot*
  countries
clerk *person who does paper work*
  in an office, bank etc.
control *checking*
Customs *I had to pay the Customs*
  £5 to import the cigarettes.

declare *say what goods you have*
duty-free *without duty (money you*
  pay to bring cigarettes, drink etc.
  into a country)
gate *Passengers for Paris go to Gate*
  12.
gift *something you give to a person,*
  a present
goods *things for sale, things a*
  person has bought
Green Channel – see page 27.
immigration *going into a country*
item *thing, piece of goods*
line *type of goods*

liqueur *e.g. Cointreau, Benedictine, Crème de Menthe*
lounge *waiting room*
luggage *baggage (suitcases, bags etc.)*
officer *e.g. a customs officer, passport officer, police officer, immigration officer*
present *something you give to a person, a gift*
purpose *the purpose of your journey = why you are travelling*
be resident in *live in*
scale *We weigh things on a scale.*
spirits (USA *hard liquor*) *e.g. whisky, cognac, vodka*
steward/stewardess (USA *flight attendant*) *man/woman who looks*

after passengers on a plane
terminal *part of an airport; Flights to Africa leave from Terminal 3.*
tobacco *Cigarettes are made from tobacco.*
transfer *change planes in the middle of a journey*
trip *journey*
twice *two times*
vaccination certificate *piece of paper saying that a doctor has vaccinated you against an illness*
valid *This is an old passport – it's not valid now.*
weight *how heavy a thing is*
wine *e.g. Riesling, Burgundy, Chianti*

Using the language

Asking if you are allowed to do things

Listen to the examples on your tape and then try to do the exercise without looking at your book. You will hear each correct answer after you say it.

1 You want to know if you are allowed to board the aircraft now.
Can I board the aircraft now?
2 You want to know if you are allowed to bring in 300 cigarettes.
Can I bring in 300 cigarettes?

You want to know if you are allowed to

- use the ticket on a weekday.
- pay by cheque.
- leave the car in London.
- break the journey in Budapest.
- catch the flight without a reservation.
- take your briefcase on the plane.

Answering questions

Listen to the question and then give
an answer beginning with *yes* or *no*.
Answer number one with *yes*,
number two with *no*, number three
with *yes* and so on.

1 Are you here on business?
Yes, I am.
2 Do you live in England?
No, I don't.
3 Have you got a visa?
4 Have you anything to declare?
5 Did you reserve a seat?
6 Are you importing any goods?
7 Is this your first visit to Norway?
8 Did you have any excess baggage?

On the aircraft

Listen to this dialogue.

Stewardess Would you like any duty-free goods?
Traveller *Yes, a litre bottle of whisky, please.*
Stewardess What sort would you like?
Traveller *Johnnie Walker, please.*
Stewardess That's $6·80.
Traveller *Can I pay in francs?*
Stewardess Haven't you got any US dollars?
Traveller *No, I haven't. I'm sorry.*
Stewardess OK, that'll be all right. I'll bring the change
in a moment.
Traveller *Thank you.*

Go back and play the role of the
traveller. Say the traveller's words at
the same time as he does. You can
look at your book if you need to.

Now go back again and this time
play the role of the traveller without
looking at your book. Stop the tape
after the stewardess's words and say
the traveller's words.

Listening for information

Now you will hear two conversations at an airport. Listen to the conversations and try to understand them without looking at the words in your book or at the Key Words on pages 21 and 22.

Conversation 1   Checking in

Check-in clerk   Good morning.

Traveller   Good morning. Can I check in here for the flight to New York?

Check-in clerk   Yes, I'm afraid it's running late today, it's leaving at ten past three instead of one o'clock.

Traveller   Oh dear.

Check-in clerk   May I have your ticket and your passport? . . . Thank you very much.

Traveller   Can I take this briefcase as hand baggage?

Check-in clerk   Yes, as long as it'll go under the seat. Have you any other baggage?

Traveller   Yes, I've got these two suitcases and this bag.

Check-in clerk   I'm afraid the baggage allowance to New York is two pieces. It doesn't involve weight, only the number of pieces.

Traveller   So how much excess baggage is there?

Check-in clerk   The extra charge is £20 for each extra piece that you have.

Traveller   For each piece above two?

Check-in clerk   Yes, so that'll be £20.

Traveller   I see. Do I have to pay now?

Check-in clerk   Yes, please . . . £20. Thank you very much. Where would you like to sit?

Traveller   No smoking, please.

Check-in clerk   No smoking. Window?

Traveller   Yes, by the window, please.

Check-in clerk   So that's 18A, that's your boarding card and your ticket that you'll need to show again at the gate.

Traveller   Thank you.

Check-in clerk   Do you have a valid visa for New York?

Traveller   Yes, I do.

Luggage
1 *Bag*
2 *Briefcase*
3 *Suitcase*

Check-in clerk Can I see it? . . . Thank you. We'll be boarding at Gate 23 at two forty-five.
Traveller Gate 23. Right, thank you very much.
Check-in clerk You're welcome.

Conversation 2
Going through Customs

Customs officer Would you like to put your luggage on here? . . . Thank you. Where have you just come from?
Traveller From Madrid.
Customs officer Madrid. Are you resident in Spain, or do you live in the UK?
Traveller I live in Spain.
Customs officer Can I see your passport, please? . . . Thank you. How long are you coming to the UK for?
Traveller For a week.
Customs officer On holiday, are you? Or business?
Traveller Yes, on business.
Customs officer I see. OK. Well then, you understand that you've come into the Green Channel, which means you have nothing to declare.
Traveller Yes.
Customs officer Is this all your luggage?
Traveller This is all, yes.
Customs officer Nobody else is travelling with you?
Traveller No, I'm travelling alone.
Customs officer OK then. What type of goods have you got, cigarettes, cigars?
Traveller I've got just 200 cigarettes.
Customs officer Nothing else at all in the tobacco line?
Traveller No.
Customs officer Any drink at all? Spirits? Liqueurs? Wine?
Traveller Just this bottle of whisky.
Customs officer Was that bought in the duty-free shop, or . . .?
Traveller Yes, at Madrid airport.
Customs officer I see. Are you bringing any gifts at all for anybody in the UK?
Traveller Well, the whisky is a present, but that's all.

1 Cigarettes
2 Cigars

Customs officer   I see. No other small items – watches,
   jewellery?
Traveller   No, it's just personal things.
Customs officer   OK. Right, sir. Would you let me have
   a look in there? . . . Is the calculator going back to
   Spain with you?
Traveller   Yes it is. It's mine.
Customs officer   Do you have a camera at all?
Traveller   No, not with me.
Customs officer   OK, sir. Thank you very much.

Go back and listen again to each
conversation until you can understand it without looking at the words.

When you understand it, read the
questions in your book. Then play
the conversation again, and stop
the tape to write the answer to each
question. Do not read the conversation
in your book when you are answering
the questions.

1   *Jewellery*
    (USA: Jewelry)
2   *Camera*
3   *Watch*
4   *Calculator*

Conversation 1

1 What time will the flight leave today?
2 What time does it normally leave?
3 What is the baggage allowance on flights to New
   York?
4 How much must she pay for the excess baggage?
5 Can she pay later?
6 What is the number of her seat on the plane?
7 Which gate will she have to go to?
8 What time will she be able to board the plane?

Conversation 2

9 Where has the traveller come from?
10 Why has he come to the UK?
11 What does it mean if he goes into the Green
   Channel?
   a) He has something to declare.
   b) He has nothing to declare.
12 How many cigarettes has he got?
13 What drink has he got?
14 Has he got any jewellery?
15 Is he going to give the calculator to another person?

Reading for information

Look at the information and then answer the questions. Use the Notes if you need to, but try to answer the questions before looking at the Notes if you can.

DUTY-FREE ALLOWANCES

If you have come from an EEC country the allowances in column 1 apply to goods obtained duty and tax-paid within the EEC. The allowances in column 2 apply if any of the goods were obtained outside the EEC or in a duty and tax-free shop, or duty and tax-free on a ship or aircraft.

If you have come from a country outside the EEC the allowances in column 2 apply.

**GOODS
to declare**

	1	**2**	
Tobacco Goods			
Cigarettes	300	200	double if you live outside Europe
or			
Cigarillos	150	100	
or			
Cigars	75	50	
or			
Tobacco	400 grammes	250 grammes	

If you have more than the duty-free allowances listed or if you have prohibited or restricted goods go into the **RED CHANNEL** and declare them to an officer.

Alcoholic Drinks		
over 38.8° proof (22° Gay-Lussac)	1½ litres	1 litre
or		
not over 38.8° proof *or* fortified *or* sparkling wine	3 litres	2 litres
plus		
still table wine	3 litres	2 litres

Persons under 17 are not entitled to tobacco and drinks allowances

**NOTHING
to declare**

Perfume	75 grammes (3 fl. oz. or 90 cc)	50 grammes (2 fl. oz. or 60 cc)
Toilet water	375 cc (13 fl. oz.)	250 cc (9 fl. oz.)
Other goods	£50 worth	£10 worth

If you have nothing more than the duty-free allowances and no prohibited or restricted goods go straight through the **GREEN CHANNEL** unless asked to stop by an officer.

and, **if you are visiting the United Kingdom for less than 6 months,** all personal effects (except tobacco goods, wine, spirits and perfume) which you intend to take with you when you leave.

1 You are arriving in the UK from Copenhagen. You
   have 75 cigars which you bought at a shop in the
   city. Will you have to pay duty?
2 You are flying from Milan to Birmingham. You want
   to buy perfume without paying duty. How much can
   you buy at the duty-free shop at Milan airport?
3 You are arriving in the UK from Montevideo, where
   you live. How many duty-free cigarettes can you
   bring in?
4 You are going to fly from Marseilles to London. You
   want to buy some Sauterne (white wine) at a shop in
   Marseilles before you go to the airport. How much
   can you take to London duty-free?
5 You are going to London for three weeks. Will you
   have to pay duty on your camera?

Now check your answers with the
Key on page 104.

Notes

alcoholic *Beer, wine and whisky are*
alcoholic drinks.
EEC *European Economic*
Community, Common Market
effects *things which belong to a*
person e.g. clothes
entitled to *allowed to have*
fl. oz. *fluid ounce (weight)*
intend *I intend to leave today*
= I am going to leave today.
obtain *buy, get*

prohibit *not allow*
proof *30% proof = 30% alcohol in*
a drink
tax *money paid to the government*
unless *if not*
within *in, inside*

1 *Perfume*
2 *Toilet Water*
3 *Sparkling wine*
4 *Fortified wine*

Writing

You are flying to Belfast on a
business trip, and you have been
given this form. Fill in the answers
on the form. Use the Notes if you
need to.

EMBARKATION CARD

Please complete in BLOCK letters

Surname (Mr./Mrs./Miss)   Maiden name

Christian names

Nationality/ Citizenship   Date of birth   Place of birth

Home address

Purpose of visit

Occupation   Employer

Date   Signature

Notes

birth *being born*
block letters *LIKE THESE*
Christian name *first name*
citizenship *nationality*
complete *fill in*
embarkation *getting on a plane or
ship*
employer *company that you work
for*
fill in (USA: fill out) *write your
name, address etc. on a form*

form *paper with questions that you
must answer*
maiden name *woman's name before
she was married*
nationality *the country you belong
to, e.g. Swiss nationality*
occupation *job*
signature *writing your name*
surname *family name*

Unit 4 At a hotel

Dialogue

Listen to the Dialogue. If you need to, you can look at the words in your book or at the Key Words after the Dialogue.
Peter and Maria Almar arrive at the Hotel International in Athens, where they have reserved a room.

Peter Good evening. My name's Almar. I reserved a double room with bathroom for three nights.
Receptionist Mr Almar. Yes, room 312. Would you like to register, please? Just fill in this form.
Peter Thank you.
Receptionist And could I see your passports, please? Thank you.
Maria How much do you charge for a double room?
Receptionist It's 1500 drachmas a night, which includes a service charge.
Maria Can we get dinner this evening?
Receptionist Yes, we're serving dinner in the Roof Garden.
Peter And what time is breakfast?
Receptionist Breakfast is from 7.30 to 9.00 in the ground-floor restaurant.
Peter And could we have a call in the morning, please?
Receptionist Certainly. What time would you like it?
Peter Eight o'clock, please.
Receptionist Very good, sir. And here's your key. Room 312.
Peter Thank you. Oh, are there any letters or telephone messages for us?
Receptionist No, sir, nothing. I'll just get a porter to take your luggage up.

Roof	Lift
Fourth floor	
Third floor	
Second floor	
First floor	
Ground floor	

Britain

Roof	Elevator
Fifth floor	
Fourth floor	
Third floor	
Second floor	
First floor	

USA

Go back and listen again to the Dialogue until you can understand it without looking at the words. Then practise saying Peter and Maria's words after them.

Key words

accommodation agency
*An accommodation agency finds
hotel rooms for people*
à la carte *each dish with its own
price (see* table d'hôte)
amount *an amount of money =
some money*
bill (USA: check) *paper that says
how much you have to pay*
call *I made a call = I telephoned.*
choice *a choice of two flights = two
flights to choose from*
complimentary *costing nothing*
disco(theque) *place where you can
dance to records*
fruit *apples, oranges, bananas etc.*
key *You need a key to open the
door.*
menu *list of things to eat in a
restaurant*

message *piece of information for
another person*
porter *person who carries luggage*
receipt *paper that says you have
paid money*
receptionist (USA: room clerk)
*person in a hotel who you ask
about rooms*
register *put your name on a list*
reserve *book, make a reservation*
serve *bring food to the table*
service charge *extra money paid for
service*
table d'hôte *one price for the whole
meal (see* à la carte)
terms *price*
unconfirmed *not agreed in writing*
VAT *Value Added Tax (tax on
goods and services in Britain)*

Using the language

Asking for things

Listen to the examples on your tape
and then try to do the exercise
without looking at your book. You
will hear each correct answer after
you say it.

1 You want a seven o'clock call.
   Could I have a seven o'clock call, please?
2 You want some French francs.
   Could I have some French francs, please?

You want	a taxi.
a seat at the back.
a weekend return to Oxford.
half a litre of oil.
a room with a shower.
your key.

Asking questions

Listen to the information and then
ask the questions.

1 There are three restaurants.
   How many restaurants are there?
2 The price is $30.
   What is the price?
3 Lunch is from 12.30 to 2.30.
4 Those postcards are 20 pence.
5 The restaurant is on the sixth floor.
6 An English breakfast is £1·75.
7 Your suitcases are over there.
8 Your room number is 425.

At an accommodation agency

Listen to this dialogue.

Clerk   Good afternoon.
Traveller   *Good afternoon. I'm looking for some
   accommodation for tonight.*
Clerk   Yes, and the name is . . .?
Traveller   *Meyer. M-E-Y-E-R.*
Clerk   What kind of accommodation do you want?
Traveller   *A single room with a bathroom, please.*
Clerk   And how much do you want to pay?
Traveller   *Well, how much will it be?*
Clerk   Would £15 be all right?
Traveller   *Yes, that'll be all right.*
Clerk   Just a moment then, please.

Go back and play the role of the
traveller. Say the traveller's words at
the same time as she does. You can
look at your book if you need to.

Now go back again and this time
play the role of the traveller without
looking at your book. Stop the tape
after the clerk's words and say the
traveller's words. Give your own
name when the clerk asks you.

Listening for information

Now you will hear a conversation in which a traveller asks about a room. Listen to the conversation and try to understand it without looking at the words in your book or at the Key Words on page 32.

Receptionist   Good afternoon, sir. Can I help you?
Traveller   Good afternoon. Have you a single room with a bathroom, please?
Receptionist   Yes, I can do a single room for you this evening. Would it only be for the one night?
Traveller   For two nights.
Receptionist   For two nights.
Traveller   How much do you charge for a room?
Receptionist   Our terms are £16·50 plus VAT, and that includes a full English breakfast, so altogether that is £18·98.
Traveller   So it's £18·98 altogether, including breakfast.
Receptionist   And VAT; yes.
Traveller   Uh-huh. That's with a bathroom, is it?
Receptionist   Yes, all the rooms have private bathroom, colour television, complimentary fruit.

Hotel room
1   *Television*
2   *Fruit*
3   *Key*
4   *Newspaper*

Hotel Inter-Continental London

Traveller And can I get dinner here?

Receptionist We do serve dinner, yes. We have a choice of three restaurants; we have the Garden Restaurant, which is on the ground floor, which has an à la carte menu and a table d'hôte menu; we have the Steakhouse, which is for a quick meal; and we also have the Room at the Top on the sixth floor, which is a disco and cabaret.

Traveller I see. Well, could I book a room for two nights then, please?

Receptionist Yes, certainly, but I'm afraid I will have to ask you for payment in advance with it being an unconfirmed booking.

Traveller So you'd like the whole amount in advance, would you?

Receptionist Yes, please. Is that all right?

Traveller Yes, that's all right.

Receptionist Would you like to register then, please? And the name is?

Traveller Ross.

Receptionist So that's Mr Ross, one single for two nights.

Traveller Right.

Receptionist And that'll be £37·96, please, Mr Ross. Thank you. 98, 100, £38, 39, 40.

Traveller Thank you.

Receptionist That's your receipt. You may have a full copy of the bill in the morning. And here's your key. That's room 125, Mr Ross, and you'll find that room on the first floor. Take the lift just to your left there up to the first floor.

Traveller Thank you very much. And what time is breakfast?

Receptionist Breakfast is from seven until ten.

Traveller Seven until ten.

Receptionist In the Garden Restaurant on the ground floor.

Traveller Uh-huh. And could I have an early call, please?

Receptionist You certainly can. What time?

Traveller At seven o'clock, please.

Receptionist   Would you like a morning paper?
Traveller   Yes, I'll have an Express, please.
Receptionist   Right. So seven o'clock early call and an
Express.
Traveller   Right. Thank you.

> Go back and listen again to the
> conversation until you can under-
> stand it without looking at the words.
> When you understand it, read the
> questions in your book. Then play
> the conversation again, and stop the
> tape to write the answer to each
> question. Do not read the conversation
> in your book when you are answering
> the questions.

1 Is there a room for the traveller?
2 Does the charge of £18·98 include breakfast?
3 Does it include VAT?
4 Does it include a private bathroom?
5 Does it include fruit?
6 Which restaurant would you go to if you didn't have
much time?
7 Why does the man have to pay in advance?
a) All the guests have to pay in advance.
b) He didn't book the room in advance.
8 How much does he have to pay altogether?
9 What does the receptionist give Mr Ross?
a) A receipt.
b) A bill.
10 What is the number of Mr Ross's room?
11 What floor is it on?
12 What time does the hotel stop serving breakfast?

> Now check your answers with the
> Key on page 104.

Reading for information

Look at the information and then
answer the questions. Use the Notes
if you need to, but try to answer the
questions before looking at the Notes
if you can.

About the Hotel

The Paris Grill À la carte or plat du jour. You are sure of a warm welcome,
good service and fine cooking.

Breakfast	7.00am – 10.00am (Sundays 7.30am – 10.30am)
Luncheon	12.30pm – 3.00pm (last orders 2.30pm)
Dinner	6.00pm – 10.00pm (last orders 9.30pm)
Cold Supper	10.00pm – 12 midnight (to order before 9.30pm)

The Athena Bar is situated on the ground floor, adjacent to the restaurant.
Our expert Barman is always ready with a word of welcome and any drink
you may require.

Weekdays	11.00am – 3.00pm, 5.30pm – 11.00pm.
Sundays	12 noon – 2.00pm, 7.00pm – 10.30pm.

Drinks are served to hotel residents and their guests at any time in the
Hotel Lounge.

Hotel Services

Doctor or **Babysitter** Please telephone the Housekeeper.

Room and Lounge Service Please use the telephone.

The Hall Porter can help you with any of these: Car Hire, Garage Facilities,
Theatre Tickets, Sightseeing, Postcards and Maps, Railway, Airline
Reservations, Cable and Mail Dispatch, Timetables, Luggage Storage,
Shopping Guides, Embassy Addresses, Valeting and Dry Cleaning,
Laundry, Church Service Details, Messages and Incoming Mail.

Telex Service 8.00am – 11.00pm. Please contact Reception.

Portable Typewriters and **Electric Razors** can be obtained from the
Housekeeper.

If you have any cause for complaint, please let us know.

For your Guidance

Travellers Cheques The Cashier's Office will gladly cash all travellers
cheques and most foreign currencies.

Personal Cheques We regret that personal cheques can be accepted only if
prior arrangements have been made or on production of your Banker's
Cheque Card.

Valuables Jewellery and articles of value should be deposited with the
Cashier's Office. The Management cannot accept any liability for loss of
valuables unless they are deposited and a receipt obtained.

Departure Visitors are kindly requested to vacate their rooms by noon on
the day of departure. *Please leave your key with the Hall Porter.*

Bedroom Key Visitors are advised to close their doors when leaving their
rooms and to deposit the key with the Hall Porter.

1 What is the latest time you can arrive in the
  restaurant for dinner?
2 Which floor is the restaurant on?
3 Where in the hotel can you have a drink at four
  o'clock in the afternoon?
4 What should you do if you are ill and need a doctor?
5 Who will help you if you want to book an air ticket?
6 Can you send a telex from the hotel at half past
  seven in the morning?
7 If you wanted to leave a very expensive camera at
  the hotel, where would you take it?
8 What is the latest time you can leave your room after
  your stay at the hotel?

Now check your answers with the
Key on page 104.

Notes

adjacent to *next to*
advise *say what it is best to do*
airline *e.g. Lufthansa, Pan Am*
am (ante meridiem) *before noon*
article of value *something that is
  worth a lot of money*
babysitter *person who looks after
  children while their parents are out*
cable *telegram*
cash a cheque *get or give money for
  a cheque*
cashier (USA: teller) *person who
  pays and takes money, e.g. in a
  bank or hotel*
cause for complaint *something going
  wrong; a reason for saying you are
  not happy with your room or the
  service*
contact *speak to*
currency *e.g. Swiss francs, American
  dollars*
deposit *leave*
dispatch *sending, posting*

embassy *The American Embassy in
  London is in Grosvenor Square.*
facilities *things that help you to do
  something, things that make
  something possible*
foreign *of other countries*
grill *cooking from above or below
  with great heat*
guidance *help*
guide *book or brochure with
  information about a place*
hall porter (USA: bell captain)
  *person in hotel who does services
  for guests and tells the porters
  (USA: bell boys/bell hops) what to
  do*
hire *pay for the use of*
housekeeper *person in hotel who
  does services for guests*
incoming *arriving*
laundry *washing clothes*
let someone know *tell someone*
liability *having to pay for something*

loss *losing something (e.g. which is stolen)*
lounge *sitting-room*
mail *letters and parcels*
noon 12 *o'clock midday*
order *ask for e.g. food or drink; last orders = the latest time at which you can order:* to order *= you can have exactly what you ask for*
plat du jour *the special meal for today*
pm (post meridiem) *after noon*
portable *which you can carry*
on production of *if you show*
reception (desk) (USA: desk) *place in a hotel where you ask about rooms*

regret *be sorry*
require *need*
sightseeing *looking at interesting things e.g. Buckingham Palace, the Tower of London*
be situated *be (in a place)*
storage *putting something in a safe place when you do not want to take it with you*
traveller's cheque – see page 50
vacate *leave empty*
valeting *looking after clothes*
valuable *something that is worth a lot of money*

1   *Electric razor*
2   *Typewriter*

Unit 5   Ordering a meal

Dialogue

Listen to the Dialogue. If you need to, you can look at the words in your book or at the Key Words after the Dialogue.

Peter and Maria Almar are having a meal at a restaurant in Athens after their first day in the city.

Waiter Are you ready to order now?
Peter Yes, I think so. Could you tell us what 'dolmadakia' is, please?
Waiter It's vine leaves stuffed with meat and onions and served with lemon sauce.
Maria It sounds delicious. I'll try that, please.
Waiter And for the main course?
Maria I'll have the chicken and rice with tomatoes.
Waiter And for you, sir?
Peter I'll have the fish and vegetable soup and the roast lamb with a salad, please.
Waiter What dressing would you like on the salad?
Peter French dressing, please.
Waiter And would you like anything to drink?
Maria I'd like some white wine. Is there a Greek wine you can recommend?
Waiter Well, the Santa Helena is very nice.
Peter Yes, a bottle of the Santa Helena then, please.
Waiter Thank you.

Waiter Everything all right, sir?
Peter Yes, thank you. That was very nice.
Waiter Would you like a dessert?
Maria Not for me, thank you.
Peter No, thank you. Just two coffees. And could we have the bill, please?
Waiter Yes, sir.

1 *Sauce*
2 *Onions*
3 *Lemon*
4 *Vine leaf*
5 *Tomatoes*

Go back and listen again to the Dialogue until you can understand it without looking at the words. Then practise saying Peter and Maria's words after them.

Key words

braise *cook slowly in a covered pan*
chicken – see page 43
cutlet *piece of meat from the neck of an animal or a piece of good meat*
delicious *tasting very nice*
dessert – see page 47
dish *food, something on the menu*
dressing *something to put on a salad, e.g. mayonnaise, French dressing (oil and vinegar)*
kidney – see below
lamb *meat from a sheep*
main course – see page 47
prepare *make*

recommend *Which hotel do you recommend? = Which hotel do you think is best for me?*
roast *cook in a hot oven*
sauté *fry quickly in a little fat*
slice *piece, e.g. a slice of bread*
sour *with a sharp taste*
stew *cook slowly in water*
stuff *fill*
be tempted by *feel that you would like to have*
waiter/waitress *man/woman who serves food at table*

1   *Mushrooms*
2   *Potatoes*
3   *Rice*
4   *Kidneys*

Using the language

Ordering food

Listen to the examples on your tape and then try to do the exercise without looking at your book. You will hear each correct answer after you say it.

1 You want to order vegetable soup.
I'll have vegetable soup, please.
2 You want to order a salad.
I'll have a salad, please.

You want to order
{
roast lamb.
chicken and rice.
a steak.
tomato soup.
a beer.
ice-cream.
}

Asking somebody to explain

Listen to the examples, and then you
ask the questions.

1 You don't know the meaning of 'zabaglione'.
Could you tell me what 'zabaglione' is?
2 You don't know the meaning of 'chicken maryland'.
Could you tell me what 'chicken maryland' is?

You don't know the meaning of
| 'pommes anna'.
| 'souvlaki'.
| 'foo yung'.
| 'sauce bearnaise'.
| 'Waldorf salad'.
| 'oeufs en cocotte'.

Chicken

Booking a table

Listen to this dialogue.

Waiter Victoria Restaurant.
Caller *Oh, hello. Can I book a table for tomorrow
evening, please?*
Waiter Certainly. What time tomorrow?
Caller *Eight thirty, please.*
Waiter And how many people is it for?
Caller *Four people.*
Waiter What name is it, please?
Caller *Larsson. L-A-R-double-S-O-N.*
Waiter Very good. We'll reserve a table for you.
Caller *Thank you very much. Goodbye.*
Waiter Goodbye.

Go back and play the role of the
caller. Say the caller's words at the
same time as he does. You can look
at your book if you need to.

Now go back again and this time
play the role of the caller without
looking at your book. Stop the tape
after the waiter's words and say the
caller's words. Give your own name
when the waiter asks you.

Listening for information

Now you will hear a conversation in which four people decide what they want to eat and then order a meal. Listen to the conversation and try to understand it without looking at the words in your book or at the Key Words on page 42.

David   Well, what about starters?
Helen   I'm going to have onion soup.
Carol   I think I'll have a salade niçoise.
Michael   What is the niçoise?
Carol   Well, it's got tomatoes in.
David   You're having onion soup, are you, Helen?
Helen   Yes.
Michael   I think I'll have that too.
David   Two onion soups and one salade niçoise. And I think I'll try the mushrooms on toast.
Michael   What about the main course?
Carol   I'll have sautéed kidneys.
Michael   Yes, they're very good.
David   So that's one sautéed kidneys.
Michael   I'll have the lamb, I think.
Helen   Well, I'm tempted by the Boeuf Stroganoff.
Carol   What is it?
Helen   Well, I think it's usually stewed or braised. And served with a little cream, I think – sour cream.
Carol   Sour cream, uh-huh.
David   What about you, Michael?
Michael   I'll probably try the lamb, but I'd like to know how they do it.
Waitress   Are you ready to order now?

Meat
1   *Duck*
2   *Beef*
3   *Veal*
4   *Pork, bacon, ham*
5   *Lamb*

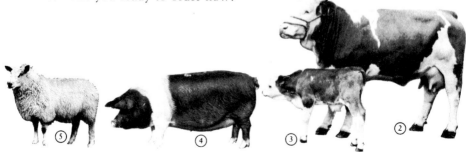

David   Yes, I think we are more or less. So to start
with, three onion soups. Is that right? Three onion
soups and one mushrooms . . .

Carol   No, sorry, I was going to have the salad.

David   Oh, two onion soups, one salade niçoise and one
mushrooms on toast. And can you tell us how some
of these dishes are prepared – the lamb for example?

Waitress   Well, the lamb cutlets are grilled and then
cooked in a sauce of wine with onions and slices
of potatoes.

Michael   Sounds delicious.

David   One lamb cutlets then.

Waitress   Would you like salad or vegetables with your
lamb? The vegetables are cauliflower, peas, carrots
or french beans.

Michael   I'll have salad, please.

Waitress   And french fries?

Michael   Please.

Helen   What did you say the vegetables were?

Waitress   Cauliflower, peas, carrots or french beans.

Carol   I think I'd like the kidneys, please. And I'd
certainly like salad.

Waitress   And french fries?

Carol   Er . . . yes, please.

Helen   The Boeuf Stroganoff – is it served with rice?

Waitress   With rice, yes. You can also have
vegetables or salad with it.

Helen   I'll have that please. And with salad.

Waitress   Boeuf Stroganoff and salad.

David   And for me steak.

Waitress   Well-done, medium or rare?

David   Medium, please. With salad and french fries.

Waitress   Did you want any wine with the meal?

Vegetables ④
1 Carrots
2 Cauliflower
3 French beans
4 Peas

French fries (chips)

Rare   Medium   Well-done

Cooked for e.g.

5 minutes   8 minutes   11 minutes

David   Yes, we do, don't we? What would we like?
Helen   Are we all going to have the same thing or . . .?
Carol   Well, David and I will probably have red wine,
and you're having beef. What about you, Michael?
Michael   Red is fine by me.
Carol   Well, there's the house wine. Shall we have a
carafe of red?
Waitress   Red wine?
Carol   Red, please.
Waitress   Thank you.

Go back and listen again to the
conversation until you can understand it without looking at the words.
When you understand it, read the
questions in your book. Then play
the conversation again, and stop
the tape to write the answer to each
question. Do not read the conversation
in your book when you are answering
the questions.

1   *Bottle*
2   *Carafe*
3   *Glass*

1   What has salade niçoise got in it?
2   What kind of soup is there?
3   Which of these is part of Boeuf Stroganoff?
   a) Sour cream.
   b) Lamb.
   c) Mushrooms.
4   What kind of sauce are the lamb cutlets cooked in?
5   What vegetables can you have with the main course?
6   Which of these is served with rice?
   a) Lamb cutlets.
   b) Sautéed kidneys.
   c) Boeuf Stroganoff.
7   One person orders a steak. Does he want it cooked
   well, medium or rare?
8   Do they order white wine or red wine?

Now check your answers with the
Key on page 105.

Reading for information

Look at the menu and then answer the questions. Use the Notes if you need to, but try to answer the questions before looking at the Notes if you can.

Two Sisters Restaurant

STARTERS

Home made soup of the day   35p
Pâté Maison with garlic toast   50p
Prawn Cocktail   75p
Mushrooms à la crême   40p
Hot prawns in wine   75p
Chilled honeydew melon & ginger   40p
Fruit juices   22p

MAIN COURSE

Roast beef "Redbridge" – thick slices of tender
beef in red wine and Dijon mustard   £2.60
Fillet steak   £3.75
Sirloin steak – tender 8-10oz steak cooked as
you like it   £3.20
Poussin en Cocotte – whole baby chicken
cooked with herbs, spring vegetables and
white wine   £2.65
Guinea fowl – cooked slowly in red wine with
bacon rolls, button mushrooms and onions and
chestnuts   £3.60
Côq au Vin   £2.10
Fresh trout – cooked with butter and almonds £1.95
Salmon steak – cooked in butter   £3.00
Side salad   45p
All served with potatoes and selection of
vegetables

DESSERTS

Sweets from the trolley   50p
Selection of cheeses   50p
Coffee, cream   25p

—— • ——

Opening times:
Wednesday, Thursday, Friday and Saturday 7.30p.m. to 10.30p.m.
Licensed restaurant.

1 Which starter is meat?
2 If you want to *eat* fruit, which starter would you have?
3 Which two main courses are chicken?
4 Which two main courses are fish?
5 Can you have rice with the main course?
6 How much is a cup of coffee?

Notes

button mushroom *small mushroom*
chill *make cold*
coq au vin *chicken cooked in wine*
fillet steak *piece of meat with no bone*
fruit juice *drink made from fruit, e.g. orange juice*
ginger *ginger has a hot taste; e.g. ginger wine, gingerbread*
guinea fowl *small bird*
herb *plant which gives food more taste*
honeydew melon *a kind of sweet melon*
licensed *allowed to serve alcoholic drinks*
oz *ounce = 28·35 grams*
pâté maison *meat paste made of e.g. liver* – see page 89
prawn cocktail *prawn with e.g. salad*
selection *a number of things to choose from*
sirloin steak *good tender piece of meat for roasting taken from near the back of the animal*
tender *easy to bite and eat*

1 Cheese
2 Melon
3 Mustard
4 Salt
5 Pepper
6 Salmon
7 Trout
8 Prawns
9 Garlic
10 Chestnuts
11 Almonds

Unit 6 Changing your arrangements

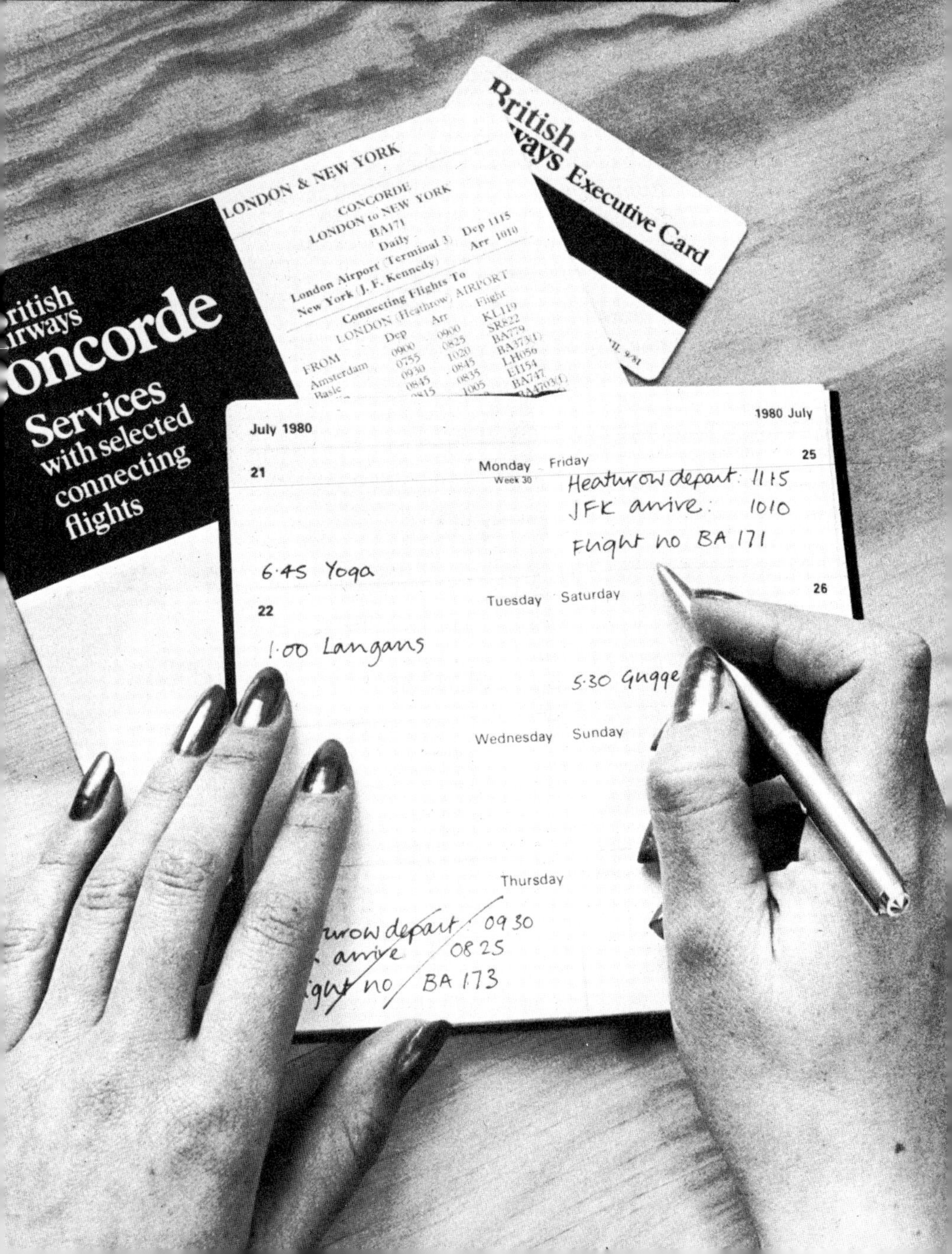

Dialogue

Peter and Maria Almar are in Athens where they are buying things for their shop in Zurich. They have got a telegram from Istanbul to say that the man they wanted to see will not be back for another week. The Almars decide to have three days' holiday in Athens and then to go back to Zurich. Maria arranges for them to stay on at the hotel.

Receptionist   Good morning.
Maria   Good morning. I wonder if we could book our room for another three nights. We were going to leave tomorrow, but we've changed our plans.
Receptionist   What's the room number?
Maria   312.
Receptionist   And how long would you like to stay?
Maria   Up to and including Sunday night, if that's possible.
Receptionist   Let me see. Yes, that'll be all right. You can keep the same room.
Maria   Thank you. And can I cash some traveller's cheques?
Receptionist   I'm sorry, we don't cash cheques, but there's a bank in the next street.
Maria   Oh, all right. Thank you.

Traveller's cheques
(USA: traveler's checks)

Maria cashes the cheques at a bank, and then Peter goes to a travel agency to re-book their flight.

Peter   I wonder if you could help me. I'd like to cancel these tickets to Istanbul and re-book to Zurich.
Travel agent   Yes, we can do that. When do you want to go?

Peter   Next Monday, please. The 17th.

Travel agent   There's just the one flight. Leave Athens 16.25, arrive Zurich 18.10.

Peter   That'll be fine.

Travel agent   I'll give you some new tickets.

Peter   Can I have a refund on the old ones?

Travel agent   I can't give you cash, I'm afraid, but I'll give you a voucher. You'll have to take it back to where you bought the tickets.

Peter   Oh, I see

Travel agent   How are you paying for the new tickets?

Peter   Will dollars be all right?

Travel agent   Certainly. They're $218 each, that's $436 altogether. Thank you very much.

Go back and listen again to the Dialogue until you can understand it without looking at the words. Then practise saying Peter and Maria's words after them.

Key words

alter *change, make different*

cancel *They cancelled the flight.
= There was no flight.*

cash *money*

change *The timetable has changed.
= The timetable is not the same as it was.*

customer *person who buys something*

different *not the same*

exchange *You pay money in exchange for goods.*

make out *write, fill in a cheque, ticket etc.*

note (USA: bill) *e.g. a £5 note*

onwards *going on, going further*

possible *Is it possible? = Can it happen?*

rate of exchange *the cost of e.g. Swiss francs in Spanish pesetas*

re-book *book again*

refund *money paid back*

sort out *find the answer (to a problem)*

stay on *stay longer*

up to and including *from Monday up to and including Wednesday (USA: from Monday through Wednesday) = on Monday, Tuesday and Wednesday*

voucher *paper which you can give for money or goods*

Using the language

Asking for help

Listen to the examples on your tape and then try to do the exercise without looking at your book. You will hear each correct answer after you say it.

1 You ask for help because you want to cancel your ticket.
I wonder if you could help me? I want to cancel my ticket.

2 You ask for help because you must see a doctor.
I wonder if you could help me? I must see a doctor.

You ask for help because	you can't find a hotel room.
	your car has broken down.
	you want to cash a Swedish cheque.
	you've lost your luggage.
	your money has been stolen.
	you don't understand the duty-free allowances.

Explaining about changes of plan

Listen to the examples and then explain why you didn't do these things.

1 Why didn't you order a taxi?
I was going to order a taxi, but I didn't have time.

2 Why didn't you book a table?
I was going to book a table, but I didn't have time.

3 Why didn't you cash a cheque?

4 Why didn't you do some shopping?

5 Why didn't you send a telex?

6 Why didn't you visit the Acropolis?

7 Why didn't you go up the Eiffel Tower?

8 Why didn't you telephone me?

At the bank

Listen to this dialogue.

Cashier Yes, please?
Customer *I'd like to buy some pounds, please.*
Cashier How many would you like?
Customer *What's the rate of exchange against the dollar?*
Cashier Two dollars and five cents to the pound.
Customer *I'll have fifty dollars' worth in pounds then, please.*
Cashier That's £24·39. How would you like it?
Customer *Five-pound notes, please.*
Cashier Five, ten, fifteen, twenty, one, two, three, four and thirty-nine pence.
Customer *Thank you.*

Go back and play the role of the customer. Say the customer's words at the same time as she does. You can look at your book if you need to. Now go back again and this time play the role of the customer without looking at your book. Stop the tape after the cashier's words and say the customer's words.

Listening for information

Now you will hear a conversation in which a traveller calls at a British Airways office. The traveller cancels his air ticket and hotel booking and re-books on a different flight.

Listen to the conversation and try to understand it without looking at the words in your book or at the Key Words on page 51.

Traveller I wonder if you can help me. I've got this ticket from Liverpool to Lisbon for 24th January, but I've changed my plans and I'm going to go to Amsterdam instead. Is it possible to cancel this ticket and change it for one to Amsterdam? I want to go on the 25th.

Booking clerk   You want to cancel the 24th and re-book on the 25th?

Traveller   Yes, re-book to Amsterdam.

Booking clerk   Is it single or return?

Traveller   Single.

Booking clerk   What time of day would you like to go?

Traveller   In the morning, please, if there's a flight.

Booking clerk   Morning. OK, I'll just check in the computer. . . . Yes, we can do a flight at 7.25 to London. Arrive in London at 8.20, then onwards to Amsterdam at 9.15. Arriving Amsterdam airport at 11.15.

Traveller   Fine. Can you alter the ticket for me?

Booking clerk   We'll give you a new one.

Traveller   Oh, thank you. And what about the money? It isn't as expensive to Amsterdam, is it?

Booking clerk   Oh, no. We'll give you a refund. Only we can't give you cash. So I'll make out a voucher for a refund, and when you get home, would you give it to your travel agents and they'll sort it out.

Traveller   Uh-huh. So can you give me the ticket to Amsterdam now without any more money from me?

Booking clerk   Yes, yes. We'll take the other ticket in exchange.

Traveller   Ah, that's fine. Another problem is that I'm booked into one of your hotels in Lisbon for two nights, the 24th and the 25th. Would it be possible to cancel that?

Booking clerk   Yes. Did you book it with your ticket?

Traveller   Yes, I did. It's a British Airways hotel, the Lisbon Penta.

Booking clerk   I'll just have a look in the computer. . . . Yes, that's OK.

Traveller   That's OK, is it?

Booking clerk   Yes, it's cancelled.

Traveller   Thank you.

Booking clerk   Right. Here's your new ticket then. Liverpool to London to Amsterdam, going on the BZ 421 at 7.25 and then London-Amsterdam on the BA 404 at 9.15. Single journey.

Cash
1   *Notes (USA = bills)*
2   *Coins*

Traveller Thank you. Where do I have to go to change planes? Do I go to the Transfer Desk?

Booking clerk No. The flight leaves from Terminal 1 and that's the terminal you arrive at, so you just go to the check-in.

Traveller So I just check in again, do I?

Booking clerk Yes.

Traveller Thank you very much.

Booking clerk I'll just make out the voucher.

Traveller Oh, yes. Thank you.

Go back and listen again to the conversation until you can understand it without looking at the words.

When you understand it, read the questions in your book. Then play the conversation again, and stop the tape to write the answer to each question. Do not read the conversation in your book when you are answering the questions.

1 What time does the flight leave Liverpool for London?

2 What time does the flight leave London for Amsterdam?

3 What does the booking clerk do?
   a) Alters the ticket.   b) Writes a new ticket.

4 Where can the traveller get his money back?
   a) At a bank.
   b) At the airport.
   c) From his travel agent.

5 Does the traveller have to pay cash for the ticket to Amsterdam?

6 Can British Airways cancel his hotel for him?

7 What are the numbers of the two flights?

8 Where does he check in when he gets to Heathrow Airport?
   a) In Terminal 1.   b) In Terminal 2.
   c) At the Transfer Desk.

Now check your answers with the Key on page 105.

Reading for information

Look at the information and then answer the questions. Use the Notes if you need to, but try to answer the questions before looking at the Notes if you can.

DINERS CLUB INTERNATIONAL

Diners Club International is not just a world-wide charge card organisation. It is also an International Club offering exclusive services to members.

THE CARD. Honoured by 400,000 establishments in 156 countries, it gives you more credit in more places than any other card—with no limit.

Travelling. Honoured by every major airline and car rental agency in the world.

Petrol. Accepted at garages displaying the Diners sign and listed in the Diners Club Motorist's Directory.

Hotels, Shopping, etc. Honoured in quality hotels, restaurants, theatres and fine stores throughout the world.

Cheque Cashing Facilities. Diners Club's association with the National Westminster Bank Group allows you to obtain up to £30 cash at any of their branches on production of your card and cheque book, drawn on any affiliated bank within the Eurocheque scheme.

Insurance. Buying any travel ticket, member and spouse are immediately covered for Loss of Life at £20,000. Members are also offered low-cost Income Protection and Accident Insurance up to £150,000.

Personal and Business Travel. Diners World Travel, a wholly owned subsidiary, offers a full travel service to members. There are also Diners Club offices in most major cities to help travellers.

Security. An optional yearly fee of 50p relieves you of all liability should you lose your card.

MEMBERSHIP. £12.50 p.a. plus a one-time entrance fee per account of £10. Supplementary members £6 when charged to same account. £75 p.a. block fee also available to Companies no matter how many members on the account.

Statements of Account. Statements are sent each month, together with copies of the original charges.

Sign your way round the world
with Diners Club International

1 In how many countries can you use a Diners Club card?
2 How much credit can you have with a Diners Club card?
   a) It depends how much you earn.
   b) As much as you like.
3 At which banks can you use the card to cash a cheque?
   a) At any bank in the National Westminster Group.
   b) At any bank in the Eurocheque scheme.
4 Which of these does the card give you free?
   a) Insurance against death while travelling.
   b) Insurance against accident.
5 If you pay extra, you will not lose money when your card is stolen. How much extra does this cost each year?
6 If you have never had a card before, how much would it cost to have a card in the first year?

Now check your answers with the Key on page 105.

Notes

account *I have an account at Barclays Bank.*
affiliated *linked with, working together with*
in association with *together with*
block fee *total charge*
branch *The bank has a branch in every town.*
charge card *credit card*
cover *The insurance covered (= included) accidents.*
directory *list of e.g. garages, hotels*
display *show*
drawn on *cheque drawn on a bank = cheque with the bank's name on it*
entrance *going in, becoming a member*
establishment *hotel, shop, garage etc.*

exclusive *exclusive services = services not given by anyone else*
fee *money paid for service*
honour *accept*
immediately *at once, without waiting*
insurance *The insurance company will pay if the luggage is stolen.*
limit *maximum amount*
major *big, important*
member *person belonging to e.g. a club*
membership *being a member*
offer *We offer cheap tickets. = You can buy cheap tickets from us.*
optional *something you can choose to do or not*
organization *company*
original *when it first happened*
p.a. *per annum, every year*

protection *keeping safe*
relieve *make free*
rental agency *company from which
  you rent (= pay to use) e.g. a car*
reverse side *other side*
scheme *system, way of organizing
  things*
security *being safe*
spouse *husband or wife*

statement *Your bank statement says
  how much you have in the bank.*
store *shop*
subsidiary *company belonging to
  another company*
throughout *in all parts of*
transferable *can be used by another
  person*

Unit 7   On the telephone

Dialogue

Peter and Maria Almar have decided
to stay in Athens for a short holiday.
Peter wants to book seats for a
concert. He is telephoning the
concert hall.

Peter Hello? Is that the concert hall?
Booking clerk Yes, speaking.
Peter I'd like to book some tickets for the concert on
Saturday, please.
Booking clerk How many would you like?
Peter Two, please. Two seats together.
Booking clerk Well, the stalls are sold out, but we have
a few in the circle.
Peter I see. What time is the performance?
Booking clerk Eight o'clock.
Peter Is there a matinée?
Booking clerk No.
Peter Well, can I book two tickets?
Booking clerk Sorry, we don't take telephone bookings.
Can you come to the box office?
Peter Oh, all right. Thank you.

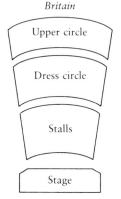

Britain

Maria wants to telephone the Almars' shop in Zurich to
tell their assistant that they will be back next Tuesday.

Maria Hello? Operator? I'd like to book a call to
Switzerland.
Operator Pardon?
Maria I want to book a call to Switzerland. I've been
trying to dial direct, but I can't get through.
Operator Can I have your number, please?
Maria Yes, it's Athens 5709–918.
Operator And who are you calling?
Maria Zurich 63 24 35.
Operator Zurich 63 24 35. And what time would you
like the call?
Maria Would it be possible to book it for three o'clock
this afternoon, please?
Operator Right. We'll call you back later, then.
Maria Thank you. Goodbye.

USA

Go back and listen again to the
Dialogue until you can understand it
without looking at the words. Then
practise saying Peter and Maria's
words after them.

Key words

box office *place where you buy
theatre tickets*
concert hall *building where music is
played*
connect *put through a call*
delay *time when you have to wait*
dial *You dial a telephone number
with your finger.*
engaged (USA: busy) *used by
another person*
expect someone back *think that
someone will come back later*
fetch *go and bring back*
hold on *wait*
matinée *performance in the
afternoon*

operator *person who puts through
telephone calls*
(I beg your) pardon? (USA: Excuse
me?) = *Please repeat what you
said; I didn't hear.*
performance *the playing of a
concert, the acting of a play etc.*
personal call (USA: person to
person) *telephone call to one
special person*
receiver *You hold the receiver when
you make a phone call.*
replace *put back*
sold out *all sold, none left to buy*
speaking *Smith speaking = I am
Smith.* (on the phone)

Using the language

Making contact on the
telephone

Listen to the examples on your tape
and then try to do the exercise
without looking at your book.

1 You are telephoning the National Theatre.
   Hello? Is that the National Theatre?
2 You are telephoning the Universal Travel Agency.
   Hello? Is that the Universal Travel Agency?

You are telephoning | the Hotel Berlin.
Kennedy Airport.
the Hong Kong Restaurant.
City Taxis.
Barclays Bank.
the police.

Asking if something is possible

Listen to the examples on your tape
and then try to do the exercise
without looking at your book.

1 You want to know if you can book a call.
   Would it be possible to book a call?
2 You want to know if you can go by bus.
   Would it be possible to go by bus?

	order a taxi.
	reserve a seat.
You want to know if you can	pay in francs.
	send a telegram.
	book a table.
	change the date of the flight.

Booking theatre tickets

Booking clerk Apollo Theatre.
Caller *Hello. I'd like to book a seat for the Tuesday evening performance, please.*
Booking clerk Stalls or circle?
Caller *Well, how much are the tickets?*
Booking clerk £4·40, £3·80 or £2.
Caller *I'll have one seat at £4·40, please.*
Booking clerk What name is it, please?
Caller *Kovalsky. K-O-V-A-L-S-K-Y.*
Booking clerk Can you come and pick up your ticket tomorrow, please?
Caller *Yes, all right. Thank you very much.*
Booking clerk Thank you.

Go back and play the role of the
caller. Say the caller's words at the
same time as she does. You can look
at your book if you need to.

Now go back again and this time
play the role of the caller without
looking at your book. Stop the tape
after the booking clerk's words and
say the caller's words. Give your
own name when the booking clerk
asks for it.

Listening for information

Now you will hear a conversation in
which someone books an
international telephone call. Listen to
the conversation and try to
understand it without looking at the
words in your book or at the Key
Words on page 61.

Operator Number, please.
Caller I want to make an international call.
Operator Which country?
Caller Iceland.
Operator I'll put you through to International.

Operator International.
Caller Hello. I want to make a call to Iceland.
Operator Can I have your number, please?
Caller Yes, it's Manchester 492 6044.
Operator 492 6044. And what number are you calling?
Caller Reykjavik 73780.
Operator Reykjavik 73780.
Caller That's right. It's a personal call to Mr Johannesson.
Operator Pardon?
Caller Johannesson.
 J-O-H-A-double-N-E-double-S-O-N.
Operator Could you replace your receiver, please, and
 I'll call you back in a few minutes.
Caller Right.

Caller Hello.
Operator Your call going to Iceland, it's still engaged,
 the number, and I'll have to give you thirty minutes
 before we try the call again. Will that be all right?
Caller Yes, that's OK. Thank you.

Caller Hello.
Operator Your call to Mr Johannesson. Is that the
 correct name?
Caller Yes, that's the name.
Operator I beg your pardon?
Caller Yes, that's the name.
Operator Trying to connect you. . . . You'll have to
 wait a little bit. Just hold on a moment. They've

gone to fetch him. . . . Hello, Manchester? Are you there?

Caller   Yes?

Operator   He's not there. Do you want to leave a message?

Caller   Well, is he expected back today?

Operator   No.

Caller   Well, could I book the call for tomorrow morning, please?

Operator   What time would you like it?

Caller   As early as possible, please.

Operator   All right, well, I'll call you back and let you know what time it'll be.

Caller   Thank you very much. Goodbye.

Go back and listen again to the conversation until you can understand it without looking at the words.

When you understand it, read the questions in your book. Then play the conversation again, and stop the tape to write the answer to each question. Do not read the conversation in your book when you are answering the questions.

1 Which country is the caller telephoning?
2 What number is he speaking from?
3 What number is he calling?
4 What is the name of the person he wants to speak to?
5 How long will it be before the operator calls back?
6 When the operator first calls back, why can't she put the call through?
   a) The number is engaged.   b) The person is not there.
7 How long will it be before she calls back again?
8 When the operator calls back the second time, why can't the caller make his phone call?
   a) The number is engaged.   b) The person is not there.
9 Does the caller leave a message?
10 What time does he want to make another call?
   a) In the morning.   b) In the afternoon.

Now check your answers with the Key on page 105.

Reading for information

Look at the information (about a
British telephone) and then answer
the questions. Use the Notes if you
need to, but try to answer the
questions before looking at the Notes
if you can.

Instructions for using a telephone in a public kiosk

To make a call

1 Lift the receiver and listen for dial tone (a continuous
purring sound).

2 Dial the number, or code and number, you want to
call.

3 Ringing tone
A repeated brr-brr sound means that the exchange is
trying to connect you to the number you dialled.

4 Call answered
When the call is answered, the tone will change to
rapid pips—immediately put a coin in the appropriate
slot and speak.

After a time you will hear the rapid pips again and if you
want to continue speaking, put another coin in the slot
at once.

5 Number engaged
If the number you have called is engaged you will hear
a regularly interrupted single tone. Replace the
receiver and try again later.

6 Number unobtainable
If you hear a continuous single tone after dialling, this
indicates the number you have called is unobtainable.
Replace the receiver—check the number, or code and
number you want and try again.

7 Operator service—dial 100
For calls which you cannot dial direct or if you have
difficulty, call the operator by dialling 100. **Do not
insert money** until the operator tells you.

SOS
To call the fire, police or ambulance emergency
services, dial 999.
Do not insert money.

1 What must you hear before you can dial?
2 What must you do when you hear rapid pips?
   a) Dial again.
   b) Put money in.
3 What does a continuous single tone mean?
   a) The number is incorrect.
   b) The number is engaged.
4 What do you dial for the operator?
5 What would you dial if you saw a bad road accident?

Now check your answers with the
Key on page 105.

Notes

ambulance *An ambulance takes
people to hospital.*
appropriate *correct*
at once *Do it at once. = Do it now;
don't wait.*
code *The code for London is 01.*
(GB: STD code, USA: area code)
continue *go on, not stop*
continuous *not stopping*
dial tone *the sound you hear before
you dial*
have difficulty *have a problem, not
be able to do something*
emergency *a situation where you
have to do something quickly e.g. a
fire*
exchange *place where telephone lines
are connected*
indicate *show*
insert *put in*
instructions *Instructions tell you
how to use something.*
interrupted *stopping, not continuous*
kiosk (USA: booth) *telephone box*
pip *a short high sound*
public *for everyone*
purring sound *the sound of a cat
when it is happy*

rapid *fast*
regular *the same each time*
repeat *say or do again*
unobtainable *cannot be used*

1 *Receiver*
2 *Dial*
3 *Slot*

Unit 8 Asking the way

Dialogue

Peter and Maria Almar are at their hotel in Athens. Maria cannot get through on the telephone to Zurich, so they want to go to the main post office to send a telegram.

Peter   Excuse me. Could you tell me the way to the main post office, please?

Receptionist   Well, it's in Aeolou Street, near Omonia Square.

Peter   Is it far to walk?

Receptionist   It's about two kilometres.

Maria   Can we get a bus from here?

Receptionist   Yes, a number twelve.

Maria   Where's the bus stop?

Receptionist   Turn left outside the hotel and go straight ahead until you get to the main road. Then turn right and the bus stop is on the right hand side opposite some shops.

Peter   I think we'll take a taxi. Could you order a taxi for us, please?

Receptionist   There's a taxi outside now, sir.

Peter   Oh, good. Thank you.
Hello, taxi? How much would it be to the main post office?

Taxi driver   Twenty-five drachmas.

Peter   OK. Could you take us there, please?

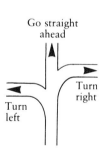

Go back and listen again to the Dialogue until you can understand it without looking at the words. Then practise saying Peter and Maria's words after them.

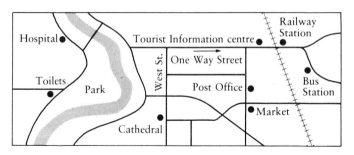

Key words

bus stop *place where you wait for a bus*

carry on *go further on the same road*

counter *A bank cashier sits behind a counter.*

inland *inside a country*

main *largest, most important*

mile = *1·61 kilometres*

motorist *person driving a car*

opposite *on the other side of the road*

overseas *in other countries*

pedestrian *person walking*

pedestrian (zebra) crossing (USA: street crossing) *place to cross the road (painted black and white)*

ring road *road going in a circle around a town or city*

roundabout (USA: traffic circle) – see page 72

sign *Road signs give drivers information.*

signposted *The station is signposted. = There are road signs showing the way to the station.*

straight ahead/straight on *forward, not turning right or left*

(set of) traffic lights *lights which tell drivers to stop or go*

turning *place where one road comes into another*

yard = *0·91 metres*

Using the language

Asking the way

Listen to the examples on your tape and then try to do the exercises without looking at your book. You will hear each correct answer after you say it.

1 You want to know where the post office is.
Excuse me. Could you tell me the way to the post office?
2 You want to know where the airport is.
Excuse me. Could you tell me the way to the airport?

You want to know	where Terminal 2 is.
	where the bus station is.
	where the National Bank is.
	where the police station is.
	where Thomas Cook's travel agency is.
	where the Air France office is.

Asking people to do things

Listen to the examples and then ask
people to do things.

1 You want a receptionist to order a taxi for you.
   Could you order a taxi for me, please?
2 You want a travel agent to cancel your booking.
   Could you cancel my booking, please?
3 You want a taxi driver to take you to the Atlas Hotel.
4 You want room service to bring you some sandwiches.
5 You want a bank cashier to change some money for
   you.
6 You want a porter to take your suitcases.
7 You want a travel agent to write down the flight times
   for you.
8 You want someone to call you back in half an hour.

At the post office

Listen to this dialogue.

Counter clerk   Yes?
Customer   *I'd like to send a telegram, please.*
Counter clerk   Inland or overseas?
Customer   *Overseas.*
Counter clerk   Can you write the address and the
   message on this form, please?
Customer   *How much is it to Italy, please?*
Counter clerk   It's 70p, plus 11p a word.
Customer   *70p, plus 11p a word.*
Counter clerk   That's right.
Customer   *Thank you.*

Go back and play the role of the
customer. Say the customer's words at
the same time as she does. You can look
at your book if you need to.

Now go back again and this time play
the role of the customer without looking
at your book. Stop the tape after the
counter clerk's words and say the
customer's words.

Listening for information

Now you will hear two conversations
in which people ask the way. Listen to
the conversations and try to
understand them without looking at
the words in your book or at the Key
Words on page 69.

Conversation 1
Asking the way on foot

Pedestrian Excuse me, I'm looking for the Tourist
Information Centre.
Woman Keep on this road.
Pedestrian This road here, yes.
Woman You'll come to another one of these pedestrian
crossings.
Pedestrian Down this way?
Woman Yes. Not this first one, the second crossing.
Pedestrian Yes.
Woman Walk over the crossing, and there's a turning
to the left. Go up there.
Pedestrian Yes, what's the name of the road?
Woman Park Street.
Pedestrian Park Street.
Woman Yes, go up there and the Tourist Information
Centre is on – is about a hundred yards up there on
the right hand side.

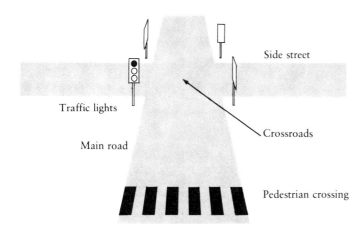

Side street

Traffic lights

Crossroads

Main road

Pedestrian crossing

Pedestrian So you go down here.
Woman Yes.
Pedestrian Cross the first crossing.
Woman But not this first crossing here.
Pedestrian Cross the second crossing.
Woman Yes.
Pedestrian And then you turn left up Park Street.
Woman Park Street.
Pedestrian And which side of the road is it on?
Woman On the right hand side.
Pedestrian Thank you very much indeed.

Conversation 2
Asking the way in a car

Motorist Excuse me, can you tell me if I'm right for the airport, please?
Man The airport.
Motorist I haven't seen any signs.
Man Yes. Just a minute. Yes, carry straight on here, straight ahead round the ring road. Go straight ahead at the first roundabout. Then there's another roundabout, go straight ahead at the next one. Then up the hill and at the third roundabout turn left. It's signposted to London. Then carry on there on that main road, and after about a mile you come to some traffic lights. You turn right at the traffic lights, it's signposted to the airport there, right at those lights, and then you carry straight along that road. There's another set of traffic lights; go straight through – straight ahead there. And then you see the airport on your right. And there's a right turn off the main road into the airport.
Motorist So it's straight ahead –
Man Straight ahead at the first two roundabouts, left at the third roundabout.
Motorist Signposted to London.
Man Right. And then right at the traffic lights and carry on another mile or two and the airport's on your right.
Motorist Thank you very much.
Man OK.

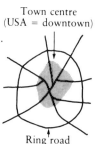

Town centre
(USA = downtown)

Ring road

Roundabout
(USA = traffic circle)

Go back and listen again to each conversation until you can understand it without looking at the words.

When you understand it, read the questions in your book. Then play the conversation again, and stop the tape to write the answer to each question. Do not read the conversation in your book when you are answering the questions.

Conversation 1

1 Where is the turning to the Tourist Information Centre?
   a) At the first pedestrian crossing.
   b) At the second pedestrian crossing.
2 Do you have to turn right or left?
3 What is the name of the street that you have to turn into?
4 How far along this street do you have to walk?
5 Which side of the road is the Information Centre on?

Conversation 2

6 At which roundabout do you have to turn off the ring road?
   a) The first.
   b) The second.
   c) The third.
7 Do you have to turn right or left?
8 What name is on the sign at the roundabout?
9 How far is it from the turning at the roundabout to the first traffic lights?
10 Which way do you go at these traffic lights?
11 Which way do you go at the next traffic lights?
12 Which side of the road is the airport on?

Now check your answers with the Key on page 105.

Reading for information

Look at the information and then answer the questions. Use the Notes if you need to, but try to answer the questions before looking at the Notes if you can.

London Transport

Buses in London are cheap, convenient, and give a frequent and comprehensive service throughout the Central area and the suburbs.

You choose your bus by the number and destination shown on the front and you can consult the detailed bus map (available at Travel Enquiry Offices and Underground stations), or the Visitor's bus map on the other side of this folder.

Most bus stops show which bus numbers stop there, give details of where the buses go and may show a map of the other stops in the area. If you are not sure which bus to catch, other people in the queue will probably be able to help you. (**Don't forget to queue up, British-style, when waiting for the bus. It's fairer for everybody**).

Getting your bus

At a 'Compulsory Stop' all buses stop.

At a 'Request Stop' you stop the bus by raising your hand in good time.

How to pay

On most London buses fares vary with the distance travelled. Unless you have a Go-As-You-Please ticket or Red Bus Rover you must pay separately for each journey; you cannot buy ordinary tickets in advance or in a 'carnet.' If you do pay for each journey, please use coins and keep your ticket until you get off the bus.

The bus conductor collects your fare on most buses, but on some (mainly in the suburbs) you enter by the yellow front doors and pay the driver. If you're not sure of the fare, say where you want to go and you will be told the cost and, if you ask, where to get off. Children under 5 travel free and those under 16 generally pay reduced fares.

1 At what kind of stop do you have to put out your
   hand to stop the bus?
2 In which parts of London are there buses?
   a) Only in the centre.
   b) Only in the suburbs.
   c) In all parts.
3 In which two of these places is there information
   about where buses go?
   a) On a bus map.
   b) At most bus stops.
   c) In the bus.
4 Is the fare always the same?
5 Where do you buy your ticket?

Now check your answers with the
Key on page 105.

Notes

carnet (French word) *book of tickets*
central area *centre*
collect *take*
comprehensive *serving all places*
compulsory *If something is
compulsory, you must do it.*
conductor *person who takes your
money on the bus*
convenient *making things easy: A
convenient bus takes you where you
want to go.*
destination *place where a journey
ends*
detailed *with full information*
distance *how far*
enter *go in*

folder *paper with information (e.g. a
map) which folds together to make
it smaller*
frequent *happening often*
generally *normally, most times*
in good time *early, not too late*
keep *not throw away*
queue (USA: line) *people
waiting in a line*
raise *put up/out*
reduced *less than the full price*
separately *not together, not at the
same time*
suburb *part of a town outside the
centre, where people live*
vary *are different, are not the same*

Dialogue

Maria Almar is going to hire a car so
that she and her husband can go on
a trip to Delphi. She is at the
Self-Drive Car Rental Company.

Maria Good afternoon.
Assistant Good afternoon, madam.
Maria I want to hire a car tomorrow. Do you have any
available?
Assistant We have a Fiat 124.
Maria How much would that cost?
Assistant It's $12 a day plus 12 cents a kilometre.
Maria And that includes insurance, presumably.
Assistant Yes, insurance is included.
Maria But I have to pay extra for the petrol, do I?
Assistant Yes, you buy your own petrol, but we check
the car and put some oil in before you start.
Maria Do I have to pay a deposit?
Assistant Yes, we require a deposit of $20.
Maria And do you accept American Express?
Assistant Yes, that'll be all right. And we need to see
your driving licence.
Maria Right. Can I see the car, please?
Assistant Certainly, madam. This way, please.

1 *Tyre*
   (USA: tire)
2 *Oil*
3 *Battery*

Go back and listen again to the
Dialogue until you can understand it
without looking at the words. Then
practise saying Maria's words after
her.

1 *Petrol*
   (USA: gas)
2 *Windscreen*
   (USA: windshield)
3 *Engine*

Key words

accident *The man was killed in a road accident.*
as well *also, too*
carburettor *Petrol and air are mixed in the carburettor.*
check *see that something is all right*
cough *You cough (= make a noise) through your mouth.*
damage *The fire did a lot of damage to the hotel.*
deduct *take away*
deposit *payment of part of the money in advance*
driving licence (USA: license) *Your driving licence shows that you are allowed to drive.*

mechanic *person who repairs cars*
mileage *the number of miles you drive*
pick up *take away*
presumably *I think, I suppose*
return *bring back*
saloon car (USA: sedan) *closed car for 4–7 people*
set off *start a journey*
third-party insurance *insurance against accidents to another person*
unlimited mileage *as many miles as you like*

Using the language

Asking to do something

Listen to the examples on your tape and then try to do the exercise without looking at your book. You will hear each correct answer after you say it.

1 You want to see the car.
Can I see the car, please?
2 You want to reserve a seat.
Can I reserve a seat, please?

You want to	sit near the front. cash a traveller's cheque. see the room. pay the bill. make a call to Venezuela. send a telegram to Kuwait.

Checking information

Listen to the information and then
say a sentence with *is it?*, *are they?*,
does it? or *do you?*. You do this to
check information and make sure it
is correct.

1 Petrol is extra.
  Petrol is extra, is it?
2 The price includes insurance.
  The price includes insurance, does it?
3 You want a deposit.
4 The service charge is 10%.
5 The meals are included.
6 You accept credit cards.
7 The allowance is 200 cigarettes.
8 The play starts at eight.

At a garage

Listen to this dialogue.

Mechanic Can I help you?
Motorist *Yes, there's something wrong with my car.*
Mechanic What's the matter with it?
Motorist *Well, it won't go very fast and the engine
makes a coughing noise all the time.*
Mechanic You've probably got dirt in the carburettor.
I'll have a look at it for you.
Motorist *You can look at it now, can you?*
Mechanic Yes, in a few minutes.
Motorist *Can I wait here, please?*
Mechanic Yes, take a seat.
Motorist *Thank you.*

Go back and play the role of the
motorist. Say the motorist's words at
the same time as he does. You can
look at your book if you need to.

Now go back again and this time
play the role of the motorist without
looking at your book. Stop the tape
after the mechanic's words and say
the motorist's words.

Listening for information

Now you will hear a conversation in which a customer arranges to hire a car. Listen to the conversation and try to understand it without looking at the words in your book or at the Key Words on page 78.

Assistant   Good morning

Customer   Good morning. I'm thinking of hiring a car next week. I want a medium-size saloon car. Do you have any cars available then please?

Assistant   Yes, we do.

Customer   What kind of cars are they?

Assistant   The cars we have are Ford Escorts or Renault 5.

Customer   How much would that cost for a week?

Assistant   For a whole week?

Customer   Yes.

Assistant   Well, the cost of the hire will be £74·50. Which includes your insurance, which is third-party insurance and damage to the vehicle.

Customer   Uh-huh.

Assistant   We also do a personal accident insurance, which is £12·40 per week, so the total cost including personal accident insurance is £86·90 for the week.

Customer   And do I have to pay something for the mileage?

Assistant   No, it's unlimited mileage.

Customer   Unlimited mileage. But I pay for my own petrol, do I?

1   *Sports car*
2   *Saloon car*
    (USA: sedan)
3   *Estate car*
    (USA: station wagon)
4   *Hatchback*

Assistant   Oh, yes. We need a £10 petrol deposit, and we fill the tank up before you set off; and then when you get back, we fill it up again and deduct the cost of that from your deposit.

Customer   Uh-huh. And I have to pay for oil as well, do I?

Assistant   No, the car is all checked and oil put in before it goes out.

Customer   And the deposit is £10.

Assistant   No, that's for the petrol. The deposit for the hire is £45.

Customer   £45. And do you accept credit cards?

Assistant   Well, not all credit cards.

Customer   Well, which ones?

Assistant   American Express, Barclaycard, Access, . . .

Customer   Good. And you need to see my driving licence, presumably.

Assistant   Yes.

Customer   Is there anything else I need?

Assistant   No, just the licence.

Customer   I see. Right. Oh, yes, about returning the car. Can I leave it somewhere else?

Assistant   No. No, we don't allow cars to be left anywhere else.

Customer   I see. Well, could I have a Renault 5 for next Monday for a week then, please?

Assistant   Yes. What name is it?

Customer   Fisher.

Assistant   And the address?

Customer   Oh. Well, I'm staying at the Royal Hotel in Baker Street.

Assistant   What's your home address?

Customer   51, Barker Road, Hong Kong.

Assistant   Well, if you'd like to pay the deposit now, and then you can pick the car up any time after eight o'clock on Monday.

Customer   Fine.

Go back and listen again to the conversation until you can understand it without looking at the words.

When you understand it, read the
questions in your book. Then play
the conversation again, and stop
the tape to write the answer to
each question. Do not read the
conversation in your book when you
are answering the questions.

1 Which of these cars does the rental company have?
a) Renault 5
b) Toyota Corolla
c) Volvo 244
d) Ford Escort

2 How much is personal accident insurance for one week?
3 Does the price of £86·90 include insurance?
4 Does the customer have to pay something extra per mile?
5 Does she have to pay for the petrol?
6 Does she have to pay for oil?
7 How much is the deposit for petrol and hire together?
8 Does the rental company accept credit cards?
a) Yes, all cards.
b) Yes, but not all cards.
c) No.

9 What does the customer need to show the company
before she can drive the car?
10 Can the customer leave the car in a different place when
she has finished with it?
11 When does she have to pay the deposit?
12 What is the earliest time on Monday morning that she
can take the car?

Now check your answers with the
Key on page 105.

Reading for information

Look at the information and then
answer the questions. Use the Notes if
you need to, but try to answer the
questions before looking at the Notes if
you can.

Terms and conditions

1 Client pays for all petrol used.
2 Cars to be returned to renting
   station.
3 State or local taxes are not
   included.
4 Driver must have a valid Driving
   Licence. Minimum age—21 years.
   For drivers under 25 years of age,
   please refer to insurance section.
5 Rates are subject to change
   without notice.
6 **Insurance**—Public Liability,
   Property Damage, $250.00.
   Deductible Collision, Fire and
   Theft is included, provided Rental
   Terms are not violated. Drivers
   under 25 years of age **must** pay
   an additional $2.50 per day for
   insurance coverage providing
   $500.00 Deductible Collision
   protection.
7 Collision Damage Waiver (CDW)
   can be purchased by drivers 25
   and over, relieving them of the
   responsibility of the first $250.00
   damage. CDW available at
   $2.00 per day.

Groups and types of vehicles

E Ford Pinto, AMC Gremlin,
   Ford Fiesta (Manual) or similar.
C Ford Fairmont, Chevrolet Nova
   or similar.
I Ford Futura, Ford Mustang or
   similar.
S Ford Thunderbird, Ford LTD or
   similar.

Notes:—
Most cars except the Ford Fiesta
have automatic gear change.

Groups C, I and S have air-
conditioning. All cars are fitted with
AM Radios.

Rates

Low Season—1st Jan —14th June,
16th Sept —31st Dec.

Group	*E	C	I	S
3 Days	$48.00	56.00	67.00	77.50
4 Days	$59.00	71.00	84.50	98.00
5 Days	$71.00	86.00	103.00	121.00
6 Days	$82.00	100.50	120.00	139.50
7 Days	$88.00	112.00	136.00	152.00
Extra Days	$13.70	17.00	21.50	23.00

High Season—15th June – 15th Sept.

Group	*E	C	I	S
3 Days	$68.50	78.50	91.00	100.50
4 Days	$80.00	94.50	114.00	120.00
5 Days	$91.00	109.50	134.50	141.50
6 Days	$103.00	124.50	150.50	161.00
7 Days	$113.00	137.00	164.50	180.50
Extra Days	$17.00	20.50	25.00	27.00

*E Car is availability basis only at some
   locations.

DOLLAR
RENT-A-CAR
SYSTEMS

1 Can you hire a car in one town and leave it in another
   town?
2 Which of these is *not* included in the rates given here?
   a) Taxes.
   b) Public liability insurance.
3 If you are over 25 and do not buy extra insurance, what is
   the most you will have to pay for accident damage?
4 How much extra does it cost per day if you do not want to
   pay for any accident damage?
5 Does the Ford Fiesta have automatic gear change?
6 Does the Ford Futura have air-conditioning?
7 How much does it cost to hire a Chevrolet Nova for 5
   days in winter?
8 How much does it cost to hire a Ford Mustang for 10
   days in August?

Notes

air-conditioning *a system that keeps
air clean and cool*
automatic *If the gear change is
automatic, you don't need to use
the gear lever.*
basis *availability basis = only when
it is available*
client *customer, person who buys or
hires something*
collision *accident*
except *We open every day except
Sunday. = Sunday is the only day
when we are closed.*
fitted with (a radio) *having (a radio)*
gear *Most cars have 4 forward
gears.*
location *place*
manual *by hand*; here: *manual gear
change*
notice *warning, telling a person
about something before it happens*
property *thing owned by someone,
e.g. a house or car*

provide *give*
provided *if*
public liability *having to pay for
accidents to other people*
purchase *buy*
refer to *look at*
renting station *place from which a
car is hired/rented*
responsibility *liability, having to pay
for something*
season *part of the year*
section *part (of a piece of written
information)*
similar *almost the same*
subject to change *may change*
theft *stealing*
violate *break*
waive *give up: Payment will be
waived. = You will not have to
pay.*

Now check your answers with the
Key on page 105.

Unit 10 Seeing a doctor

Dialogue

Peter and Maria Almar are back in
Athens after their trip to Delphi.
Peter has got a bad cold, and he has
gone to see a doctor.

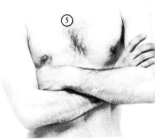

Peter I've got a very bad cold, Doctor. My head aches
and I've got a sore throat, too.
Doctor Do you get colds very often?
Peter Well, I had a cold about two months ago, and I
had a chest infection afterwards. The doctor gave me
some antibiotics.
Doctor And did you complete the course of
treatment as directed?
Peter Oh, yes.
Doctor Have you had any fever?
Peter No, no fever.
Doctor Have you had any other symptoms, such
as a cough?
Peter No, but I had a cough last time.
Doctor Was there any mucus coming up?
Peter Yes, it was white in colour.
Doctor White but not yellow or green?
Peter That's correct.
Doctor Have you had a stomach upset or any
diarrhoea?
Peter No, my stomach is all right.
Doctor I see. Well, I can give you some medicine to
unblock your nose and to ease the pain in your
throat. I think the cold will clear up in a day or two.
Peter All right. Thank you.

1 Ear
2 Mouth
3 Tooth
4 Neck
5 Chest

1 Medicine
2 Tablets

Go back and listen again to the
Dialogue until you can understand it
without looking at the words. Then
practise saying Peter's words after
him.

Key words

ache *hurt all the time*
antibiotic *e.g. penicillin*
appetite *wish to eat*
basis *on a regular basis = regularly*
(e.g. three times every day)
blocked *full: You cannot breathe*
through a blocked nose.
chemist (USA: druggist) *person who*
sells medicine
clear up *get better*
colicky *colic = short sharp pain in*
the stomach
a couple of *two*
course of treatment *treating an*
illness (helping to make it better)
over a period of time
diarrhoea *going to the toilet very*
often
as directed *as someone tells you to*
do
drug *medicine*
ease the pain *make the pain less bad*
fever *the body being too hot*
health *in good health = not ill*

infection *illness*
mucus *Mucus comes from your nose*
when you have a cold.
nauseated *feeling that you want to*
be sick
now and again *sometimes*
otherwise *in other ways*
pain *something hurting*
patient *person who sees a doctor*
prescription *a note from a doctor to*
say what medicine someone needs
recurrent *happening often*
sore *giving pain*
squeeze *press together tightly*
stomach *Food goes into your*
stomach.
such as *e.g., for example*
symptom *A symptom shows that*
you are ill.
upset *Too much rich food gives you*
an upset stomach/a stomach upset.
vomit *be sick, bring up food from*
the stomach
while *period of time*

Using the language

Saying what is wrong with you

Listen to the examples on your tape
and then try to do the exercise
without looking at your book. You
will hear each correct answer after
you say it.

1 You are seeing a doctor about a sore throat.
I've got a sore throat.
2 You are seeing a doctor about a bad cold.
I've got a bad cold.

You are seeing a doctor about
| a cough. |
| a headache. |
| a stomach upset. |
| toothache. |
| diarrhoea. |
| earache. |

Talking about the past

Answer the questions using the word *yesterday.*

1 When did you book the tickets?
I booked the tickets yesterday.
2 When did you buy the camera?
I bought the camera yesterday.
3 When did you cash the cheque?
4 When did you have a cold?
5 When did you reserve the table?
6 When did you arrive in Mexico?
7 When did you make the phone call?
8 When did you see the doctor?

At the chemist's

Chemist Can I help you?
Customer *Have you something for a headache, please?*
Chemist Is it for you?
Customer *Yes, I've got a bad headache.*
Chemist Try these tablets. They're very good.
Customer *What are they?*
Chemist Aspirin. Take two every four hours.
Customer *Two every four hours.*
Chemist That's right.
Customer *Yes, I'll have them, please.*

Go back and play the role of the customer. Say the customer's words at the same time as she does. You can look at your book if you need to.

Now go back again and this time play the role of the customer without looking at your book. Stop the tape after the chemist's words and say the customer's words.

Listening for information

Now you will hear a conversation in
which a patient sees a doctor. Listen to
the conversation and try to understand
it without looking at the words in your
book or at the Key Words on page 87.

Patient Good morning, Doctor.
Doctor Good morning. Sit down, please. Now what can I
do for you?
Patient Well, I live in Germany, but I'm staying here in
England for a week. I've been here two days now, and
I've got an upset stomach.
Doctor How long ago did your stomach upset begin?
Patient Just after I arrived here – about two days ago.
Doctor So you've had it for a couple of days?
Patient Mm.
Doctor When you say you've an upset stomach – have you
lost your appetite?
Patient A bit, yes. If I eat, my stomach gets upset
afterwards.
Doctor Do you feel nauseated?
Patient No, not really.
Doctor You haven't vomited?
Patient No.
Doctor Do you have any
pains now and again?

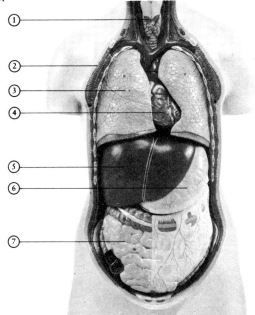

1 Throat
2 Muscle
3 Lung
4 Heart
5 Liver
6 Stomach
7 Intestine

Patient   Mm. I get pains quite often.
Doctor   Is it an aching type pain or is it a colicky pain –
squeezes and lets go.
Patient   Yes, a colicky pain.
Doctor   And when you have the pain, have you had any
diarrhoea?
Patient   Yes, a little bit. I usually have to go when I have the
pain.
Doctor   How often do you have to go?
Patient   About four or five times a day.
Doctor   And after you've had the diarrhoea, is the pain
eased – at least for a while?
Patient   For a while, yes.
Doctor   Hmm. And then comes back again. Has there been
any blood with the diarrhoea?
Patient   No.
Doctor   Have you had any problems like this before?
Patient   Only when I'm travelling.
Doctor   But it's not a recurrent problem?
Patient   I don't get it often, no.
Doctor   Have you had any fever?
Patient   No.
Doctor   Have you had any other symptoms such as a sore
throat or a cough?
Patient   Not this time, no.
Doctor   Not in the last couple of days?
Patient   No.
Doctor   Do you happen to know if you've eaten anything
unusual that has upset you before?
Patient   No, I don't think so. But I eat in restaurants a lot
when I'm travelling of course.
Doctor   Mm. Your general health is otherwise good?
Patient   Yes.
Doctor   And you're not taking any sorts of medicines
on a regular basis?
Patient   No.
Doctor   No. Well, this is simple traveller's diarrhoea. It
usually clears up in a very few days. I'll just give you
something for the diarrhoea.
Patient   I see. Fine.
Doctor   I'll give you a prescription.
Patient   What should I do with it?

Doctor You just go to the nearest chemist. Give it to him. He'll ask you for a small prescription charge, but there's no charge for the drug itself.
Patient I see.
Doctor And then you take it as directed. And that will be written on the bottle.
Patient Right.
Doctor And if it doesn't get better, you can come back – but it will.
Patient OK. Thank you very much.

Go back and listen again to the conversation until you can understand it without looking at the words.

When you understand it, read the questions in your book. Then play the conversation again, and stop the tape to write the answer to each question. Do not read the conversation in your book when you are answering the questions.

1 What is wrong with the patient?
2 Does he feel sick?
3 Does he have a pain in his stomach?
4 How often does the patient have to go to the toilet?
5 Does he have this problem when he is *not* travelling?
6 Is he normally in good health?
7 What illness has the patient got?
8 How soon will he be better again?
9 What does the doctor give the patient?
10 Who should the patient give it to?
11 Will the patient have to pay any money before he can have the medicine?
12 Who or what will tell the patient how often he must take the medicine?
   a) The doctor.
   b) The chemist.
   c) The bottle.

Now check your answers with the Key on page 106.

Reading for information

Look at the instructions for taking
Alka-Seltzer tablets and then answer
the questions. Use the Notes if you
need to, but try to answer the
questions before looking at the Notes
if you can.

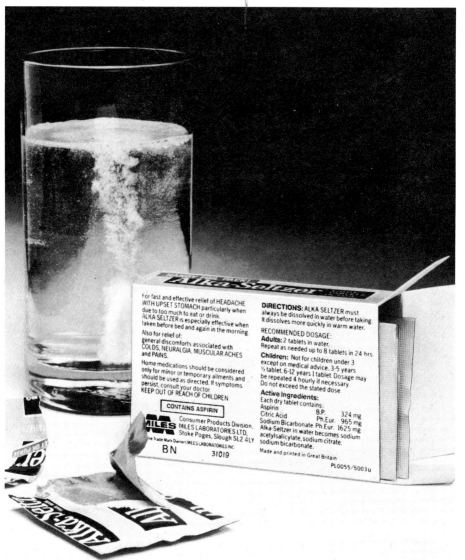

For fast and effective relief of HEADACHE
WITH UPSET STOMACH particularly when
due to too much to eat or drink.
ALKA-SELTZER is especially effective when
taken before bed and again in the morning.
Also for relief of:
general discomforts associated with
COLDS, NEURALGIA, MUSCULAR ACHES
and PAINS.

Home medications should be considered
only for minor or temporary ailments and
should be used as directed. If symptoms
persist, consult your doctor.
KEEP OUT OF REACH OF CHILDREN

CONTAINS ASPIRIN

Consumer Products Division,
MILES LABORATORIES LTD,
Stoke Poges, Slough SL2 4LY
The Trade Mark Owners MILES LABORATORIES INC

BN   31019

DIRECTIONS: ALKA SELTZER must
always be dissolved in water before taking.
It dissolves more quickly in warm water.
RECOMMENDED DOSAGE:
Adults: 2 tablets in water.
Repeat as needed up to 8 tablets in 24 hrs.
Children: Not for children under 3
except on medical advice. 3-5 years
½ tablet. 6-12 years 1 tablet. Dosage may
be repeated 4 hourly if necessary.
Do not exceed the stated dose.
Active Ingredients:
Each dry tablet contains:
Aspirin   B.P.   324 mg
Citric Acid   Ph.Eur.   965 mg
Sodium Bicarbonate Ph.Eur. 1625 mg
Alka-Seltzer in water becomes sodium
acetylsalicylate, sodium citrate.
sodium bicarbonate.
Made and printed in Great Britain
PL0055/5003u

1 Which one of these would you take Alka-Seltzer for?
   a) A fever.
   b) A headache.
   c) A sore throat.
2 How do you take a tablet?
   a) You put it in your mouth and then drink a little water.
   b) You put it in water first and then drink the water.
3 How many tablets do you take at one time?
4 How many tablets can you take in one day?
5 How many tablets can an 8-year-old child take at one time?
6 Can you give Alka-Seltzer to a baby?

Now check your answers with the Key on page 106.

Notes

ailment *illness*
associated with *part of*
consider *think about*
consult *talk to*
contain *The bottle contains medicine.* = *There is medicine in the bottle.*
directions *instructions: The directions tell you how to use something.*
discomfort *not feeling well*
dissolve *become like water: Salt dissolves in water.*
dose/dosage *how much medicine you take*
due to *because of*
effective *An effective medicine makes you better.*
especially *more than usual: Drive carefully, especially at night.*

heartburn *burning feeling in the chest after eating*
ingredients *the ingredients of a medicine* = *what is in the medicine*
on medical advice *if a doctor tells you*
medication *taking medicine*
minor *small*
muscular *in the muscles: You use your leg muscles when you run.*
necessary *needed*
neuralgia *pain in the face and head*
particularly *especially: London is very crowded, particularly in summer.*
persist *not stop*
relief *pain going away*
temporary *happening for only a short time*
up to *up to six* = *six or less, but not more than six*

Dialogue

Peter and Maria Almar are looking
round the shops in Athens before
they catch the afternoon flight back
to Zurich. Maria is looking for a
pair of shoes.

Maria Excuse me. Do you speak English?
Assistant Yes, madam. Can I help you?
Maria I'm looking for a pair of blue shoes to wear
with a dress.
Assistant Blue.
Maria Yes, you've got some in the window at 1450
drachmas. Could I try them on, please?
Assistant What size is it?
Maria 38.
Assistant Just a moment, please. Yes, here we are.
Maria Are they leather?
Assistant Oh, yes.
Maria I like the style.
Peter Yes, they're very nice.
Assistant Do they fit all right?
Maria They feel a bit tight actually. Have you a larger
size?
Assistant We haven't got that shoe in a 39, I'm afraid.
Maria Have you anything similiar in blue that would
fit me?
Assistant No, we haven't. I'm sorry.
Maria I'll leave it then. Thank you very much.

1 *Shoes*
2 *Sandals*
3 *Boots*

Go back and listen again to the
Dialogue until you can understand it
without looking at the words. Then
practise saying Maria's words after
her.

Key words

accessible *easy to find*
shop assistant (USA: sales
  clerk) *person who serves customers
  in a shop*
bottom *bottom shelf = shelf
  below/under the other ones*
carpet *You put a carpet on the floor.*
cotton *Clothes made of cotton are
  cool to wear. We get cotton from a
  plant.*
crystal *The best glass is crystal.*
department store *large shop selling
  many different things*
document *paper, certificate*
fit *be the right size*
identity *who a person is*
leather *We get leather from the skin
  of an animal, e.g. a cow.*
matter *it's a matter of = you have to*

overcoat *coat to keep you warm*
plastic *A plastic handbag is cheaper
  than a leather one.*
process *do the things that need to be
  done*
raincoat *coat to keep you dry*
serve *help a customer*
silver *shiny white metal*
size *how big something is*
style *what something looks like*
tight *fitting too closely, too small*
top *The lift went all the way up to
  the top floor.*
try on *put on clothes to see if they
  fit*
wood *We get wood from trees.*
wool *We get wool from sheep.*

Using the language

Asking what things are made of

Listen to the examples on your tape
and then try to do the exercise
without looking at your book. You
will hear each correct answer after
you say it.

1 You want to know if the shoes are made of leather.
  Are these shoes leather?
2 You want to know if the glass is made of crystal.
  Is this glass crystal?

You want to know if	the carpet is made of wool.
	the trousers are made of cotton.
	the handbag is made of leather.
	the chairs are made of wood.
	the shirt is made of cotton.
	the coffee-pot is made of silver.

Explaining what you want

Listen to the examples, and then
explain what you want.

1 This coat is too heavy.
  This coat is too heavy. Have you anything lighter?
2 These glasses are too small.
  *These glasses are too small. Have you anything
  bigger?*
3 This jacket is too long.
4 This table is too low.
5 The colour is too dark.
6 These shoes are too wide.
7 This box is too big.
8 This camera is too expensive.

Buying things

Listen to this dialogue.

Assistant Are you being served?
Customer *No, I'm not. How much are these glasses?*
Assistant They're £8·50 for a box of three.
Customer *I'll take two boxes, please.*
Assistant That's £17, please.
Customer *And can I have a carrier bag, please?*
Assistant It's 5p for a plastic bag.
Customer *Yes, I'll have one.*
Assistant That's £17·05 altogether. Thank you.
Customer *Thank you.*

Go back and play the role of the
customer. Say the customer's words
at the same time as he does. You can
look at your book if you need to.

Now go back again and this time
play the role of the customer without
looking at your book. Stop the tape
after the assistant's words and say
the customer's words.

Listening for information

Now you will hear a conversation in
which a customer at a department store
in the UK arranges to export goods and
get back the money he has paid in tax.

Clerk   Can I help you?
Customer   Yes, please. I've bought these two coats and
these sweaters, and I want to take them back to
Brazil with me. Can I get the money back that I've
paid in tax?
Clerk   When did you arrive in the UK?
Customer   It was 14th February.
Clerk   14th February. And you're leaving when?
Customer   Next Tuesday.
Clerk   Next Tuesday. That's 6th March. Oh, well,
that's fine. And you're not a British resident?
Customer   No, I live in Brazil.
Clerk   Well, it's just a matter of filling in this form.
Your passport and identity document, if I could see
that. . . . Thank you. Could I have your home
address in Brazil?
Customer   Yes, the address is on this card here.
Clerk   Thank you. And now if I could have your
receipts, please. Two sweaters. Are they men's
sweaters or ladies'?
Customer   Men's sweaters.
Clerk   What colour are they?
Customer   Well, this one in here's blue, and this one's
brown.
Clerk   Blue sweater and a brown sweater.
Customer   And I've got these two coats.
Clerk   Two coats.
Customer   One grey and one brown.
Clerk   And those are ladies' coats are they, or men's?
Customer   They're both men's.
Clerk   Both men's, yes. Both overcoats, or raincoats?
Customer   Overcoats.
Clerk   Both overcoats.
Customer   Yes.

Clerk And then if you'd sign it here. . . . Now then, we'll give you this stamped addressed envelope. I'll put the receipts that you've given me in with this. Now when – as you go through Customs, you must go through British Customs, give them this form and the receipts and if necessary have your goods accessible so that they can see them, going through.

Customer So I give this form with my receipts to the Customs.

Clerk To the British Customs on your way out of the country.

Customer Yes.

Clerk They'll give you one copy back and keep one themselves.

Customer Uh-huh.

Clerk So – there will be a postbox quite near – so if you – the copy that they give you – if you will send it back to us in the stamped addressed envelope, then we'll process it as soon as it comes back.

Customer So the Customs takes one copy.

Clerk The Customs take the bottom copy, and they give you this top copy.

Customer And I post that back to you.

Clerk You post that back to us.

Customer What about the receipts? Do I keep them?

Clerk Oh, you keep the receipts.

Customer I see. And how long will it take for the money to arrive?

Clerk Well, we usually get the form back within two or three days of you leaving the country, so within four or five days of you leaving the country we've sent the cheque off to you.

Customer So you'll send the cheque to my home address?

Clerk Yes.

Customer I see. Well, thank you very much.

Go back and listen again to the conversation until you can understand it without looking at the words.

1 *Envelope*
2 *Stamp*
3 *Address*
4 *Postbox*
   (USA: mailbox)

When you understand it, read the
questions in your book. Then play
the conversation again, and stop the
tape to write the answer to each
question. Do not read the conversation
in your book when you are answering
the questions.

1 When did the customer arrive in the UK?
2 When is he leaving?
3 Where does he live?
4 How many sweaters has he bought?
5 Has he bought men's coats or ladies' coats?
6 Where does the customer have to show the form and
receipts?
a) At a post office.
b) At British Customs.
c) At Customs in his own country.
7 When he gets back a copy of the form, what must he
do with it?
a) Send it to the department store.
b) Keep it.
8 Who keeps the receipts for the goods?
9 How soon after the customer's departure will the
cheque be posted to him?
a) In two or three days.
b) In four or five days.

Now check your answers with the
Key on page 106.

Reading for information

Look at this notice in a department
store and then answer the questions.
Use the Notes if you need to, but try
to answer the questions before
looking at the Notes if you can.

BASEMENT

China   DIY   Household   Radio & Electrical
Shoe repairs   Snack bar   Wall coverings

GROUND FLOOR

Clocks & Watches   Cosmetics   Fashion accessories
Foodhall   Hosiery   Jewellery   Lingerie   Luggage
Perfumery   Photography   Toiletries   Wine shop

FIRST FLOOR

Bank   Books   Children's wear   Customer accounts
Haberdashery   Linens   Magazines   Men's wear
Pharmacy   Stationery   Tobaccos   Travel bureau   Wools

SECOND FLOOR

Fashion fabrics   Footwear   Ladies' fashions
Men's toilets   Millinery   Public telephones
Restaurant

THIRD FLOOR

Floorcoverings   Furnishings   Furniture   Hairdressing
Sports   Toys   Women's toilets

Which floor would you go to for each of these things?

1 a pair of men's trousers	7 a postcard
2 a television	8 a dress
3 some aspirins	9 a bed
4 a carpet	10 a pair of shoes
5 some tomatoes	11 a handbag
6 a camera	12 a present for a 3-year-old boy

Notes

Basement *the floor under the ground floor*

children's/men's wear *clothes for children/men*

china *cups, plates, glasses etc.*

cosmetics *face-cream etc., make up*

D.I.Y. *do-it-yourself (paint, nails etc.)*

fashion accessories *gloves, handbags etc.*

fashion fabrics *cotton, silk, wool etc. for making clothes*

fashion *(women's) clothes*

footwear *shoes, boots etc.*

furnishings *curtains, cushions, fabrics for the home*

furniture *chairs, tables etc.*

haberdashery (USA: notions) *needles, cotton, things for sewing*

hairdressing *cutting and washing hair*

hosiery *socks, stockings, tights etc.*

household *things for the kitchen*

linens *table-cloths, bed sheets etc.*

lingerie *underclothes, nightwear etc. for women*

magazine *e.g. 'Time', 'Newsweek'*

millinery *hats*

pharmacy (USA: drugstore) *chemist's*

repair *This watch is broken – it needs repairing.*

snack *quick meal*

stationery *paper, envelopes etc.*

toiletries *things for the bathroom*

toy *Children play with toys.*

Now check your answers with the
Key on page 106.

1   Dress
2   Jacket
3   Trousers
      (USA: pants)
2+3   Suit
4   Coat
5   Vest
      (USA: undershirt)
6   Pants
      (USA: shorts)

7   Hat
8   Sweater
9   Scarf
10   Gloves
11   Jeans
12   Blouse
      (USA: shirtwaist)
13   Skirt
14   Shirt
15   Shorts

Key

Unit 1

Listening 1 Six o'clock   2 Eight o'clock   3 Two
4 £32   5 Wash-basin, shower and toilet.
6 £36   7 Twelve   8 Couchette   9 £25·80
10 Yes   11 Yes   12 No   13 b)   14 Yes

Reading 1 £30·50   2 £26   3 a)   4 Full fare   5 9.45

Unit 2

Listening 1 A monthly return   2 £24·55   3 On the return
journey   4 19.00   5 About £4   6 Monday
7 Saturday   8 The return journey

Reading 1 44 lbs (20 kgs)   2 c)   3 c)   4 22   5 b)
6 Y.D. 35   7 Y.D. 15   8 10·45

Unit 3

Listening 1 3.10   2 1.00   3 Two pieces   4 £20
5 No   6 18A   7 Gate 23   8 2.45   9 Madrid
10 On business   11 b)   12 200   13 A bottle of
whisky   14 No   15 No

Reading 1 No   2 50 grammes   3 400   4 3 litres   5 No

Unit 4

Listening 1 Yes   2 Yes   3 Yes   4 Yes   5 Yes   6 The Steakhouse   7 b)   8 £37·96   9 a)   10 125
11 The first floor   12 Ten o'clock

Reading 1 9.30 pm   2 The ground floor   3 In the
Lounge   4 Telephone the Housekeeper   5 The Hall
Porter   6 No   7 To the Cashier's Office
8 Noon/Midday/12 o'clock

Unit 5

Listening 1 Tomatoes 2 Onion soup 3 a) 4 A sauce of wine 5 Cauliflower, peas, carrots or french beans 6 c) 7 Medium 8 Red wine

Reading 1 Pâté Maison 2 Melon 3 Poussin en Cocotte and Coq au Vin 4 Fresh trout and salmon steak 5 No 6 25p

Unit 6

Listening 1 7.25 2 9.15 3 b) 4 c) 5 No 6 Yes 7 BZ 421 and BA 404 8 a)

Reading 1 156 2 b) 3 a) 4 a) 5 50p 6 £22·50

Unit 7

Listening 1 Iceland 2 Manchester 492 6044 3 Reykjavik 73780 4 Johannesson 5 A few minutes 6 a) 7 30 minutes 8 b) 9 No 10 a)

Reading 1 The dial tone 2 b) 3 a) 4 100 5 999

Unit 8

Listening 1 b) 2 Left 3 Park Street 4 About 100 yards 5 On the right 6 c) 7 Left 8 London 9 About a mile 10 Right 11 Straight ahead 12 On the right

Reading 1 A Request Stop 2 c) 3 a) and b) 4 No 5 In the bus

Unit 9

Listening 1 a) and d) 2 £12·40 3 Yes 4 No 5 Yes 6 No 7 £55 8 b) 9 Her driving licence 10 No 11 Now 12 Eight o'clock

Reading 1 No 2 a) 3 $250 4 $2 5 No 6 Yes 7 $86
8 $239·50

Unit 10

Listening 1 He has an upset stomach. 2 No 3 Yes 4 Four or
five times a day 5 No 6 Yes 7 Traveller's diarrhoea
8 In a very few days 9 A prescription 10 A chemist
11 Yes 12 c)

Reading 1 b) 2 b) 3 Two 4 Eight 5 One 6 No

Unit 11

Listening 1 14th February 2 6th March 3 Brazil 4 Two
5 Men's 6 b) 7 a) 8 The customer 9 b)

Reading 1 First 2 Basement 3 First 4 Third 5 Ground
6 Ground 7 First 8 Second 9 Third 10 Second
11 Ground 12 Third

Wordlist

The numbers tell you on which page there is a picture or an explanation giving the meaning of the word.

dress *103*
dress circle *60*
dressing *42*
driving licence *78*
drug *87*
druggist *87*
drugstore *102*
duck *44*
due to *93*
duty-free *21*

E

each way *3*
ear *86*
ease *87*
economy class *12*
EEC *28*
effective *93*
effects *28*
elevator *31*
embark *18*
embarkation *29*
embassy *38*
emergency *66*
employer *29*
engaged *61*
engine *15, 77*
enquire *3*
enter *75*
entitled to *28*
entrance *57*
envelope *99*
especially *93*
establishment *57*
estate car *80*
exceed/in excess *9*
except *84*
exchange *51, 66*
exclusive *57*
excuse me *61*
expect someone back
  61

F

fabrics *102*
facilities *38*
fare *3*
fashion accessories *102*
fashions *102*
fee *57*
ferry *3*
fetch *61*
fever *87*
fillet steak *48*
fill in/out *29*
fit *96*
fitted with *84*
flight *3*
flight attendant *22*
floor *31*
fl. oz. *28*
folder *75*
following *3*
foreign *38*
form *29*
formalities *18*
fortified wine *28*
french beans *45*
french fries *45*
frequent *75*
fruit *34*
fruit juice *48*
furnishings *102*
furniture *102*

G

gallery *60*
garlic *48*
gas *77*
gate *20*
gear *84*
general information *9*
generally *75*
gift *21*

ginger *48*
glass *46*
gloves *103*
goods *21*
in good time *75*
Green Channel *27*
grill *38*
ground floor *31*
guidance *38*
guide *38*

H

haberdashery *102*
hairdressing *102*
hall porter *38*
ham *44*
hard liquor *22*
hat *103*
hatchback *80*
health *87*
heart *89*
heartburn *93*
herb *48*
hire *38*
hold on *61*
honeydew melon *48*
honour *57*
hosiery *102*
household goods *102*
housekeeper *38*
hoverport *9*

I

identity *96*
immediately *57*
immigration *21*
include *3*
incoming *38*
indicate *66*
infant *18*
infection *87*